International Journal of Social Science Research and Practice (IJSSRP)

Vol. 1, Nos. 1 and 2
September 2013

"An Interdisciplinary Journal"

Department of Sociology and Criminal Justice
Virginia State University
Petersburg, VA 23806

ISSN 2162-9307 (Print)
ISSN 2162-9293 (Online)

Because of the dynamic nature of the Internet, any web addresses or links contained in this book may have changed since publication and may no longer be valid. The views expressed in this work are solely those of the author and do not necessarily reflect the views of the publisher, and the publisher hereby disclaims any responsibility for them.

Any people depicted in stock imagery provided by Thinkstock are models, and such images are being used for illustrative purposes only.
Certain stock imagery © Thinkstock.

International Journal for Social Science Research and Practice (IJSSRP)
Vol. 1, Nos. 1 and 2   September 2013

Editor
Zacchaeus Ogunnika

International Journal for Social Science Research and Practice (IJSSRP)
Vol. 1, Nos. 1 and 2   September 2013

Contents

International Journal for Social Science Research and Practice (IJSSRP)

Mission Statement

International Journal for Social Science Research and Practice (*IJSSRP*) is an interdisciplinary peer-reviewed journal. The objective of the journal is to serve as a forum for the exhibition and dissemination of scholarly activities in forms of current researches and thoughts on contemporary issues. The scope of *IJSSRP* is wide and all-inclusive as it ranges from issues in the United States to global events and happenings. It welcomes all types of researches ranging from field and experimental to rigorous theoretical explanations. It welcomes empirically based studies and discussions based on abstractions and theoretical understanding. *IJSSRP* will serve as the forum for the promotion of positive exchange between nomothetic and idiographic traditions in the social sciences.

The journal is independent of any particular school of thought and does not lean toward any theoretical perspective or viewpoint. Authors are not limited by their nationality, religion, subject matter, or theoretical orientation. The journal is, however, interested in studies that will promote global unity and understanding toward achieving a peaceful global village, global social harmony, and economic growth. It therefore promotes studies that can yield practical solutions to contemporary global social problems.

SUBMISSION GUIDELINES

IJSSRP is an international journal, which appears in printed and online forms, and it is published quarterly. Authors should recognize the unbiased posture of the journal in political, social, and cultural issues and respect *IJSSRP*'s quest for sound and rigorous intellectual discourse. Authors should submit their manuscripts by e-mailing to the editor at zogunnika@vsu.edu and by following the submission instructions.

Authors who cannot e-mail their manuscript should store them on a modern removable storage device (jump drive, disc, etc.) and send it to the editor along with three hard copies mailed to:

International Journal for Social Science Research and Practice (IJSSRP) Attention: Dr. Zacchaeus Ogunnika Department of Sociology and Criminal Justice Virginia State University, Petersburg P. O Box 9036, VA 23806, USA

Manuscripts should be in Microsoft Word files. Word perfect or any other file types will not be accepted. The files should not be PDF read-only files.

Authors should make sure that their manuscripts are well edited for language, typos, and other errors. Manuscripts should be double spaced, justified to the left and right, and twelve-point font of Times New Roman format should be used. Headings should be twelve-point bold Times New Roman and should not be underlined. Use bold italics rather than underlines for emphasis. Tables and figures are encouraged and welcome, but they should be well arranged and used when and where necessary.

Authors are responsible for the accuracy of their references. Submissions should follow any of the following publication formats: ASA, APA, and MLA for reference, style, and guidelines.

Keep to one style of publication manual. Papers should be of adequate length of not more than twenty pages excluding references. Book reviews should be of a length between 700 and 1,950 words. Authors should note that minor editorial changes can be effected on their papers, if necessary.

The Kiwanis Club and Its Educational and Volunteering Outreach: Insights from Social Exchange and Social Control Theories

Egerton Clarke, Ph.D.
Kent State University

ABSTRACT

This paper was undertaken to examine current common practices among Jamaican Kiwanis Club members involved in educational outreach and volunteerism, to assess the relationship between formal education and volunteerism, and to assess the role that volunteerism may play in creating opportunities for paid employment. Data were drawn from conversations with three active members of the Kiwanis Club in Jamaica. Results suggest that members volunteer mainly because of a desire to assist individuals in need, to develop and maintain enriched social contacts, and to promote community development through fund-raising. The paper recommends a more inclusive approach to recruiting club members—an approach that would not only attract more females but would narrow the gender gap at the leadership level.

INTRODUCTION

This paper discusses the effectiveness of volunteerism by students and graduates who join the Kiwanis Club. The author recognizes that the Kiwanis Club reaches out to help meet the needs of people who face various challenges including those in mental institutions and nursing homes and that through its fund-raising drives, many understaffed and ill-equipped hospitals have been able to meet the needs of their communities. Therefore, this paper is specifically attuned to the club's school-based and community volunteerism. The paper argues that for Jamaica to move forward, its graduates must go beyond the expectation for tangible economic rewards. Nation-building requires shared responsibility from its graduates. One of the ways by which students and graduates are contributing to community development is through volunteerism as promoted by the Kiwanis Club.

By the turn of the twenty-first century, most academic degree-holding Jamaicans were first-generation college or university graduates. This means that they were the first members of their immediate families to have graduated from an institution of higher learning. Apart from the time of graduation ceremony, many parents of graduates had never walked the halls of college or university buildings. And yet the parents of first-generation university students are very knowledgeable and accomplished in the school of life itself. They know how to work hard and to be satisfied with modest means. It would be a mistake to think that such hardworking, engaged citizens are not educated. Nevertheless, when we speak of "educated people," we usually conjure up notions of formal academic preparation and accomplishment. Although educational attainment is both formal and nonformal, and in spite of the importance of the latter, for the purpose of this paper, it is the former that deserves priority over the latter. This priority is warranted especially because of Jamaicans' unrelenting quest for higher education since the 1970s.

Over the past three decades, Jamaica has been expanding opportunities for higher education, both locally and abroad. In 1995, the University of Technology, formerly the College of Arts, Science, and Technology, was formally accorded university status. Similarly, Northern Caribbean University, formerly West Indies College, was accorded university status in the 1990s. These two universities have joined the University of the West Indies, Mona Campus, in offering undergraduate- and graduate-degree programs. Additionally, the island's teacher-training colleges, the College of Agriculture, Science and Education, the United Theological Seminary, and several other private institutions are now offering baccalaureate and some graduate-degree programs. One main goal is to equip graduates with skills and knowledge for personal and community development.

In spite of the growing number of institutions of higher learning and increased enrollment, the demand for teacher-training diplomas, bachelors, and graduate training exceeds the capacity of local colleges and universities to deliver. Consequently, offshore universities are intensifying their recruitment drives to take advantage of Jamaicans' search for higher education. For example, hundreds of Jamaicans are pursuing undergraduate and graduate programs from several universities in Florida, Texas, Georgia, South Carolina, North Carolina, and New York. These institutions offer courses in Jamaica, and students fulfill residency requirements in the United States during the summer. At the same time, thousands of other Jamaican students are pursuing full-time studies at these and other universities in the United States, Canada, United Kingdom, Russia, Germany, France, India, and Cuba.

This drive for higher learning has far-reaching benefits to the scholars themselves and for community development in general. For example, we know that higher education provides greater opportunities for higher incomes. People with above-average incomes are twice as likely as low-income people to describe their health as excellent. People with more wealth live, on average, seven years longer because they eat more nutritious foods, live in safer and less stressful environments, and receive better medical care (U.S. National Center for Health Statistics, 1999). However, higher education seems unattainable for a large number of Jamaicans who live in poverty. Herein lays the role of the Kiwanis Club, a charitable organization that has been paving the way for less fortunate children to succeed. The club realizes that the long road toward university graduation begins with the first step. Hence, much of the club's volunteering activities are geared toward nurturing and strengthening academic excellence from the early stages of the child's life.

There is a plethora of studies dealing with volunteerism in general, but there has been little research that focuses on the link between the reciprocal role of formal education, volunteerism, and social control. The role of the Kiwanis in this endeavor adds a special dimension that is not known before.

In the first part of the paper, the author explicates the social exchange theoretical perspective as an approach to framing the discussion. This is followed by a description of the Kiwanis Club and an investigation into the benefits of volunteering. The discussion then draws upon Hirschi's model of social control theory to assess the extent to which volunteerism can lead individuals to build important attachments to significant others and thus conform to conventional norms and behaviors. In the final section, the inquiry turns to the question: how can other individuals be motivated to volunteer? Recommendations are made for a more inclusive approach to recruitment and greater opportunities for females to assume leadership roles within the club.

THEORETICAL BACKGROUND

VOLUNTEERISM AND SOCIAL EXCHANGE THEORY

In order to gain a better understanding of the reciprocal exchange between volunteers and beneficiaries, it is helpful to consider Peter Blau's (1964) work *Exchange and Power in Social Life*. This model of social exchange relations between human beings has its parallel in economic markets, a type of exchange and reciprocal relations that is empirical, rational, and sometimes calculating. That is, people expect at least a rough equality between what they give and what they receive. They judge actions by their results, and a sense of strain or injustice will arise if there is a serious imbalance between what one gives and what one receives in return. The exchange may be delayed rather than immediate. Delayed reciprocity means that we forgo immediate gratification with the expectation that rewards will be forthcoming at some future time (Clarke, 2001). This view of social exchange is in synch with one of the emerging global trends about volunteerism. Merrill (2006) draws attention to one such trend, the recognition of the role and importance of reciprocity, community, social solidarity, and citizenship.

DATA AND METHODS

Three participants were conveniently selected from different chapters of the club. They were informed about the ethical conditions under which they would participate. All three interviewees were males. Face-to-face conversation-like interviews took place in the interviewees' homes and lasted for about one hour each. Open-ended questions dominated the interviews, and interviewees were allowed to talk freely about the activities and practices of the club.

THE KIWANIS CLUB

Driven by its motto, "Help a child today and you help an adult/nation tomorrow," the Kiwanis Club operates several chapters throughout the fourteen parishes of Jamaica. Its programs are based on the belief that helping one child can make a big difference to the society as a whole. By helping a child through school, the club enhances the child's productivity and, by extension, the productivity and development of the society as a whole. Help is offered through education at all levels. The club provides grants to needy students from the primary level to the tertiary level. Average club membership is about thirty. Each club holds weekly meetings as well as regular interclub meetings. Clubs are judged by their performance in fund-raising and community activities. Hence, interclub meetings not only keep members informed about the various activities around the country; they create opportunities for friendly rivalry in terms of performance.

Females are underrepresented both in terms of membership and in leadership levels of the club. It must be noted, however, that at one time, Jamaica had a female as governor of the club.

Children are introduced to the club in their early teens. They form a branch called Key Club. The senior club attracts members from later teens to adulthood. The age distinction notwithstanding, members from both branches of the clubs regularly interact, especially at interclub meetings (see discussion below). Interclub meetings are important ways by which the Kiwanis Club creates opportunities for intergenerational relationships. Through this link between young and old, older members teach and mentor the young and thereby inspire a sense of volunteerism early in life.

Like the family, the school, the church, the mass media, and the government, the Kiwanis Club constantly points children to education as the gateway to upward social mobility. Through its volunteering activities, the club makes the pathway to the top of the social ladder more accessible to underrepresented children in Jamaica. It gives needy children a chance to pursue higher education, and it facilitates their continued development.

LESSONS FROM THE KIWANIS CLUB INTERNATIONAL

Volunteering is a trait that is popular with the Kiwanis Club worldwide. As a result of the generosity of the Kiwanis Club, many students stay in school instead of living a life on the streets or at the shopping malls. Mentoring initiative is high on the list of priority of the club. The club's operation in Jamaica is no different from the work that goes on internationally. Club members in Jamaica leave behind a track record of selfless volunteerism that has rescued children from street life. Volunteers are richly rewarded when, through their mentoring, students stay in school. Mentoring outcomes include high completion rates and reduced dropouts. Volunteers help students by caring and by guiding them through appropriate methods of conflicts resolution.

The mentoring program involves a meaningful two-way exchange relationship between participants and beneficiaries. Club members develop and sustain such projects like drug awareness-teen challenge, prayer breakfast, feeding street people, mentoring young at-risk boys, read across Jamaica, and youth basketball. These projects are indicative of the big difference the Kiwanis Club is making in Jamaica.

WHY DO INDIVIDUALS VOLUNTEER?

Volunteerism does not mean to take on boring tasks. Neither does it mean that volunteers get nothing in return. When asked, "Why do club members volunteer?" response included, "The truly educated citizens volunteer because our work is worth much more than money can buy," "We volunteer because helping a child through school is a worthwhile project to undertake," "We like to volunteer because of the mental stimulation and social challenge involved." The most common response was "We volunteer because of the feelings of fulfillment in seeing a child succeed in school." Despite the many hours and other costs involved, volunteers consider caring as a major source of motivation. Monsignor Gregory Ramkissoon (2011) shares this view by declaring at a recent Stella Maris fund-raiser that "we find ourselves when we lose ourselves in the care of others" (cited by Jean Lowrie-Chin, "The Power of Volunteerism," Opinion Section of *The Daily Observer*, available on July 11, 2011, at www.Jamaicaobserver.com).

Apart from the psychological, intangible benefits that giving entails, there are other practical ways by which volunteerism is rewarded. Mary V. Merrill (2005) shares these benefits in her book *Ten Professional Development Benefits of Volunteering (Everything I Learned in Life I Learned through Volunteering)*. According to Merrill (2005), these benefits include learning or developing a new skill, thus making one more marketable, and connecting to one's community and achieving a sense of fulfillment and balance in one's life.

PRACTICAL BENEFITS OF VOLUNTEERING

This means that the giving of time and funds leads to a two-way exchange whereby the beneficiaries tend to avoid being passive recipients of others' benevolence and are inclined to reciprocate. By reciprocating, they avoid being categorized as victims who are not in control of their lives and in need of help. Loseke (2003) notes that we do not blame the victims for their plight, but within the cultural theme of individualism that prizes self-sufficiency and individual control, victims are failures. The identity of victim is claimed more often by people who are powerless. Hence, the benefits of volunteering stir the volunteers to keep on volunteering. Forward (1994) suggests that the amount of volunteering increases because once volunteers experience it; they find it difficult to ignore a plea for help again. There comes a time when the recipient feels an urge to give back by helping someone, the school, or the community in general.

The spirit of volunteerism that emanates from members of the Kiwanis Club is a two-way exchange relationship that involves reciprocity. This exchange is commonly viewed by the saying, "You scratch my back, and

I'll scratch your back." By helping to equip a basic school, by purchasing books and other supplies for needy children, club members are scratching the itchy backs of young Jamaicans. In return, beneficiaries scratch the backs of volunteers when the fruits of volunteerism turn a would-be dropout into a bright scholar; or when by lending a helping hand, a health care facility is able to serve the community. A club member's back is scratched in return when the charity activities of the club stem the flow of young girls becoming "women of the night." Mutual back scratching goes on when students stay in school, when they successfully complete academic programs, and when club members and members of the wider community feel safe from crime.

In times of lean economic situations, people tend to save and spend less, and this may seem understandable. However, Merrill (2005) cites research showing that among two hundred of the leading businesses in the United Kingdom, 73 percent of employers would recruit a candidate with volunteering experience over one without, 94 percent of employers believe that volunteering can add to skills, 94 percent of employees who volunteered to learn new skills had benefitted either by getting their first job, improving their salary or being promoted. This is a source of motivation for graduates who are challenged by unemployment in lean economic times. Although economic downturn often runs hand in hand with declining financial contributions to charities, volunteerism has steadily increased (Forward, 1994). Knowing that volunteering creates employer-driven opportunities, graduates who join the Kiwanis Club realize that they attract the attention of employers.

The Kiwanis Club is helping to promote academic success and community development all across Jamaica as seen from the value of time spent volunteering to mentor school children, the pleasant smile on the face of the child who was helped with the term's school fees, the expressed gratitude of the teachers for providing sanitary convenience and library resources, the help given to needy children who lack guidance in skills and character building, tutoring at-risk children, and the joy on the face of an orphan after being offered a nourishing meal at the canteen. The club is contributing to the achievement of the school and ultimately to the development of the community. It appears that employers are more likely to hire a person they perceive as being a good community citizen because of her or his volunteerism.

While social exchange theory helps us to understand the two-way flow of rewards between volunteers and beneficiaries, taken alone, it does not appear to adequately account for the success of the Kiwanis Club in promoting volunteerism, social integration, and conformity to conventional norms. A fuller picture of volunteerism may be afforded by drawing on the basic premise of social control theory as well.

VOLUNTEERISM AND SOCIAL CONTROL THEORY

Hirschi's (1969) view of social control helps us pose important questions about social integration and ways by which volunteerism can lead to this. Hirschi (1969) conceptualized social integration as a set of social bonds between individuals and conventional society. Rather than trying to discover why individuals engage in deviance (or crime), Hirschi (1969) posed the question: Why don't people commit delinquent acts? In the context of this paper, social unrest in schools or delinquency does not go hand in hand with acts of volunteerism by students. Successful students who are involved in acts of volunteerism or mentoring programs are not the ones called to the vice principal's office to answer charges of playing hooky, school yard fights, or poor academic performance. Reciprocal volunteerism is somewhat like symbiotic interdependence among the school, the home, and the community. This case is made clearer by the popular view that it takes a village to raise a child. Schools that are supported by charitable clubs and organizations are more successful than schools where these clubs are absent. Like Hirschi (1969) then, the questions may be: Why do students and graduates volunteer? Why do volunteers promote community development?

Hirschi (1969) identifies four social bonds:

- attachment—the intensity and variety of interests a person has in common with others in the community
- commitment—reflected in the amount of energy a person expends on community-oriented activities

- involvement—indicated by the person's expenditure of time on projects of common interest
- belief—the acceptance of a common system of values and moral precepts

Hirschi concludes that the stronger the bonds between individuals and conventional social life, the less likely they would engage in deviant behavior.

VOLUNTEERISM AS A TECHNIQUE FOR CRIME CONTROL

During the last twenty or more years, the quests for higher education and increase in crime and violence have been moving upward together. While this correlation is not necessarily causal, it is worth looking into. Given the steady rise in crime and violence in Jamaica, it is compelling to consider the role of the Kiwanis Club in promoting security and social control.

Nowadays, many Jamaicans are asking the question, "Why do people commit crime?" Many scholars have been asking the same question for years. In some ways, a similar question is being asked here: How can the Kiwanis Club help poor, at-risk individuals accept common values and societal norms to structure their behavior? Answer to this question may be found in Hirschi's (1969) model of social control. In their "Report on Building Active Citizens," Grimm et al., (2006) argue that fostering environments that encourage volunteer activities are critical for creating a commitment to service and community involvement that will remain with them for their lifetime. The Kiwanis Club is actively working with Jamaican families, religious organizations, and schools to promote values of volunteerism especially on behalf of children at risk. By promoting academic achievement and volunteerism, the club is building social and economic integration of young Jamaicans. Given the success of the Kiwanis Club then, Hirschi's (1969) question seems relevant: Why do the youngsters conform? Success requires that youngsters are kept engaged in conventional activities to the extent that they have little or no time left for unconventional or criminal activities. The mentoring program fosters a sense of commitment toward community development. It creates opportunities for partnership and common interests, and it encourages shared values and beliefs all of which lead to social conformity.

RECRUITMENT AND RETENTION OF MEMBERS

A narrowing of the gender gap may pose a unique challenge to the Kiwanis Club in Jamaica where, historically, gender role socialization has favored male dominance in terms of numbers and leadership role. Merrill (2006) identifies the importance of pluralistic approaches to recruitment, engagement, and management as one of the six volunteering patterns that are emerging globally. Jamaica can benefit from a more inclusive approach that will narrow the gender gap in membership and put more females in management positions. Joanne (2006) discusses what she considers the "top ten ways to recruit and engage youth volunteers." These ways include: (1) developing teamwork by encouraging group participation and let volunteers learn from each other; and (2) finding adults to work with young volunteers that they can identify with. Graduates have specific skills and experience that are not commonly found elsewhere. It is helpful then for the Kiwanis Club to harness the resources of graduates who have passed through the mentoring process. They can be a source of motivation to new mentees. Continued success may require that the club encourage participation from all levels, including parents, elderly persons, and past students of local schools. This broader base of support is likely to enhance retention and promote sustainability of programs.

LIMITATIONS

This paper has focused on the Kiwanis Club, but other charitable clubs like the Rotary Club and the Lions Club are promoting volunteerism in Jamaica. Rotarians are no stranger to volunteerism in Jamaica. Hence, the success of schools and mentoring of students cannot be exclusively attributed to the work of the Kiwanis Club. Instead, the Kiwanis Club is a partner in the promotion of volunteerism.

RECOMMENDATIONS

One way to increase recruitment and retention is to let volunteers feel that they can make a meaningful contribution to their community. It is important to let them feel that they have certain rights and responsibilities including the rights to a job that is worthwhile and challenging, be trusted with necessary confidential information, be kept informed of what is happening in the organization, be given appropriate recognition even on a day-to-day basis, and be treated as nonpaid staff members. Similarly, the volunteer should have responsibility to know her or his limit, respect confidential matters, follow organizational guidelines, prepare for each work assignment, acknowledge the need for training, participate fully, and work as a team member.

FINAL THOUGHTS

The Kiwanis Club is one of a cornerstone of nation-building in Jamaica. The projects that they are working on testify that the club is a shining example of the spirit of volunteerism. Based on insights from social exchange theory, we learn from respondents that volunteerism and other outreach activities are richly rewarded through a domino effect. Seen from social control theory, the club is playing a vital role in promoting social integration and community development. However, the gains and promises made by successful mentoring of students are being threatened by the rapid and concurrent growth in crime and violence and poverty. These challenges can stir club members and policy makers into further action. Success will depend on careful planning for recruitment and retention of members and recognition of rights and responsibilities of volunteers.

REFERENCES

Blau, Peter. 1964. *Exchange and Power in Social Life*. New York: Willy.

Forward, David. 1994. *Heroes After Hours: Extraordinary Acts of Employee Volunteerism*. Jossey-Bass, Inc., San Francisco: California

Fritz, Joanne. 2006. *Top Ten Ways to Recruit and Encourage Youth Volunteers*. Retrieved from http://nonprofit.about.com/od/volunteers/tp/recruityouth.htm

Grimm, Robert, et al., 2006. *Building Citizens: The Role of Social Institutions in Teens Volunteering*. Retrieved from http://www.worldvolunteerweb.org/resources/research-reports/national/doc/building-active-citizens-the-1.html

Hirschi, Travis. 1969. *The Causes of Delinquency*. Berkley: The University of California Press.

Loseke, Donileen R. 2003. *Thinking About Social Problems: An Introduction to Constructionist Perspectives*: New York: Aldine de Gruyter.

Merrill, M. (2005, October 19). *Ten Professional Benefits*. Retrieved from http://www.worldvolunteerweb.org/resources/how-to-guides/volunteer/doc/benefits-of-volunteering.html Merrill, Mary. 2006. Global Trends and the Challenges for Volunteering. *The International Journal of Volunteer Administration*, 24(1), 9-14.

U.S. National Center for Health Statistics, 1999.

The Christian Missionary Agencies And Western Education In Igboland: A Study Of The Primitive Methodists In Amauzam, 1921-2010

Dan O. Chukwu, Ph.D.
Department of History and International
Studies, Nnamdi Azikiwe University, Awka, Nigeria

ABSTRACT

Among the factors that influenced the course of events in Nigeria during the colonial period was the institutionalisation of Western education via the school system. The system came along with the spreading of Christianity, first in the southern part of the country, and much later, attempts were made at evangelising the northern region. Even in the north, where Islam and Arabic education appear to have taken root earlier, the influence of Western education was to be dominant. In this paper, attempts are made to chronicle the role of the Christian missionary agencies—the Primitive Methodist Mission and the Roman Catholic Mission—in the introduction of Christianity and Western education in the Nkanu area of Enugu State. The paper uses as a case study, Amauzam, a village in Ugbawka town of the present Nkanu East Local Government Area. It underscores that despite the introduction of formal education there in the early years of the twentieth century by the missionary agencies, the village and indeed the Nkanu clan may not have fared well in terms of high manpower development. The paper blames this ugly development on a number of factors including the missionary agencies themselves and the colonial government. It, however, suggests various ways to stem the ugly trend.

INTRODUCTION

The influence of Western education has been profound on the individuals, groups, and societies that have been opportuned to have access to it. But in an attempt to gain access to Western education, sometimes these individuals and groups no doubt would have paid some prices which include denial of some immediate temporal and temporary pleasures. In colonial Africa, where the mode of capital formation was at its lowest ebb, parents and guardians were known to have mortgaged landed property and other valuables to be able to send their children and wards to school—if only they would be like the *Oyibo* man in dressing and speaking the white man's language. But beyond dressing and speaking the white man's language, those who acquired functional education in our own clime are known to have over time had a head start over others. They sometimes do not possess as much material resources as the other members of their community, yet they seem to be the leading lights wherever they are found. They are patrons of the saints and ambassadors of peace; they are also the spokespersons of their communities. These are the ones who understand the usefulness of the pen believed to be mightier than the sword. It is, therefore, the issue bordering on manpower development that this paper examines. The paper has been divided into a number of sections, including the location of our study area on the Nigerian map, the nature, the introduction of Western education in Amauzam, and the ways to mobilize for formal education. The paper has relied more on both primary (oral interviews) and secondary source material.

CONCEPTUAL DEFINITIONS

In this paper, a number of words completely un-English have been used by the researcher. Within the present context where the essay is written in English, there is a compelling need to define these words to enable the non-Igbo-speaking reader to understand the researcher's worldview. These words include the following:

Agbaja: The term "Agbaja" is used here to refer to both a clan and a geographical area. As an area, the Agbaja clan is an area west of Enugu

Urban and stretches to Nsukka as well as expands westward toward the Anambra Valley. As a group, the Agbaja possesses dense population and is divided into six subclans: Umu Neke, Umu-Osie Akulu or Umu Ezeagu, Umu-Ojebe-Ogene, Umu-Ngwunye, and Ngwo. At present, the Agbaja constitutes the Udi and Ezeagu Local Government Areas in Enugu State, Nigeria

Amadi: Used by the Igbo in general to refer to the free-born members of the society.

Amauzam: This is the study area of the paper. It is one of the villages that constitute Ugbawka. According to an oral source, Amauzum village was founded by Agbushi, the son of Iwana (an itinerant warrior).

Nkanu: The origin of the word "Nkanu" has remained controversial among the people. However, the reality of the Nkanu clan in constituting a major factor in Igbo social and political setting goes back to the emergence of Chief Jim Nwobodo and Chief Ken Nnamani on the Nigerian political space. As an economic group, the Nkanu is known to possess large, rich, and arable land for agriculture; hence, before and after the introduction of colonial rule, they continued as great farmers. As an Igbo clan, Nkanu is comprised of several towns and villages. The Nkanu is found in Enugu East, Enugu North, and Enugu South Local Government Areas. They are also found in Nkanu East and Nkanu West Local Government Areas of Enugu State.

Obia: This is used as a subtle way of referring to the strangers or slaves in the Igbo society. The other Igbo versions of Obia are Ohu or Oru.

Oborka: This is a corruption of the word Ugboka by the Europeans at the beginning of their conquest of Igboland. At some other times, the Europeans wrongly spelt and anglicized the word as Ugbawka. It may interest the reader to note that throughout this paper, we have adopted the anglicized version of the word.

THE NATURE AND ELEMENTS OF EDUCATION

The concept, education, may deem to possess different meanings to different folks. While to some it may mean a better way of living, to others it is the process of teaching required skills. Yet to some group of boys and girls (and perhaps even men and women now reflecting on their childhood experiences at school), education is an unpleasant memory, especially when they recall the teacher's cane and the bully of their seniors. Perhaps these are just few of the layman's conceptualization of education. On the other hand, the understanding in some circles is that education is a socialization process which has something to do with the transmission of cultural values such as traditions, customs, norms, and the belief system from one generation to another. In fact, according to a renowned American sociologist, Margaret Mead (1943), education is believed to be somewhat synonymous with socialization. By this definition, she means that education is the cultural process, the way in which each newborn human infant is transformed into a full member of a specific human society. This, perhaps, is the type of education most people, whether they went through a formal school setting or not, did imbibe from their parents or siblings.

On his part, James B. Stroud (1946) gives a broader understanding of education; hence, he says that it is the process by which societies perpetuate or renew themselves. By extension, Stroud is of the view that education begins for a man or woman whenever they first interact with the other members of the society—an interaction, he further maintains, could shape and condition their behaviour.

When taken together, however, these definitions lack a fulfilment of our expectation for this paper as they tend to suggest a continuous and inseparable relationship between the individual and the society. This is a kind of continuous socialization. The process of education here is informal and to a large extent, possesses the potentials for the fulfilment of the requirements of African traditional education, viz:

(a) Respect for the elders and constituted authorities;
(b) Healthy attitude toward honesty;

(c) Sense of membership and participation in family and community affairs;

(d) Development of the child's latent physical skills for labor (Nwachuku, 1990).

Seen in the light of the foregoing, it may be argued that every African possesses some level of education, yet not everyone is literate. Thus, education, in the context of this paper, refers to the Western/formal education.

WHAT IS WESTERN/FORMAL EDUCATION?

In view of the fact that education as a socialization process does not fulfill professional expectations, sometimes it may not have met the requirements of the international society. In all honesty, respect for one's elders and constituted authorities, as our traditional education teaches us, may not be a prerequisite for landing a good job as an accountant, a teacher, a doctor, or even as a clerical officer. Each of these positions and many others require some formal training.

It may, therefore, be important to state here that when we speak of formal education, we invariably underscore a school system in which designated persons are expected to impart certain types of acceptable behavior and profession to the pupils and students. This normally requires the development of human intellect for the upliftment of the human society. This may be what F. Harbison and C.A Meyers (1964), two of the most twentieth-century American scholars, describe as functional education. It is that education that possesses the potent force for transforming the human society into a heaven on earth. Harbison and Meyers further describe this as human resource, the engine room for the societal growth and development. According to them, human resource development is a process of increasing the knowledge, the skills, and the capacities of the people in a society with a view to promoting its economic, social, and political growth (Harbison and Meyers, 1964, Todaro and Smith, 2003:394-396).

At this point, we may think of how the human mind works when the potency of formal education has been acquired. We may think of how the Nigerian nationalist leaders of the twentieth century, armed with the power of formal/functional education, were able to dismantle the vestiges of British colonialism; and in their place, they were able to enthrone political independence in 1960. In this respect, the thinking of great minds like Benjamin Nnamdi Azikiwe, Christopher Akweke Abyssinia Nwafor Orizu, and Jeremiah Obafemi Awolowo on functional education and the freedom of man may be relevant. For instance, Orizu did not stop at his philosophy of horizontal education (Orizu, 1994: Chapters 18-23; Chukwu, 2004: Chapter 9). He rather translated his idea into a reality when he floated his American Council on African Education (ACAE) in the 1940s and 1950s to foster scholarships for young Africans to study in the American universities and colleges. Many young men and women of the period were known to have thus benefited from the scholarship scheme. An outstanding example of the many beneficiaries was Professor Babs Aliu Fafunwa, once Nigeria's Education Minister (Orizu 1994). In addition to the scholarship scheme in 1959, Orizu founded the Nigeria Secondary School, Nnewi, in an attempt to equip young Nigerians to face their future squarely. The motto of that college was "To educate the mind is to liberate it."

On his part, Awolowo, as premier of the defunct Western Region of Nigeria, launched a free education scheme (in the 1950s) for the education of the Westerners. That singular policy of the period had its effect on the region as in the subsequent years (and till date) the southwest geopolitical zone of the country has continued to lead the country in terms of manpower cum economic development (Oladesu and Yishau, 2010:3). These explanations assume that where there are other resources, including cash for trading, without the coordinating effort of the trained manpower, development may be void. It takes human agents to mobilize capital, to create markets, to carry on trade, and to manufacture cars and refrigerators.

Given that it takes human agents to mobilize and allocate other resources of the society, it may be necessary to appreciate the relevance of functional education. There can, therefore, be no gainsaying the fact that any society that denies its citizens the right to formal education has denied them a fundamental human right. In much the same way, any citizens of a country that shun the right and opportunity to basic education may have condemned themselves perpetually to a state of ignorance, savagery, and backwardness. In Nigeria, for instance, although not much has been done to translate the various policies on educational development into a reality, at least some theoretical framework has been set out in this direction. Accordingly, in chapter 2 of the country's 1989 Constitution, Section 14, Subsection 3, the government is expected to provide, when practicable, free education at all levels.

EARLY CONTACT OF IGBOLAND WITH WESTERN INFLUENCES

Historical studies have shown in that while the coastal people of Calabar, Warri, Badagri, and Lagos, among other West Africans, might have been exposed to the influences of the European predators as far as the fifteenth century AD, their counterparts in the hinterland had to wait for the next three hundred years or so, to be so "blessed." In the Igbo country, especially the northern Igbo area, W. B. Baikie, one of the earliest European adventurers to visit this part of West Africa, made a reflection of his encounter with the Igbo in 1854 in the following words:

> *In Igbo, each person hails, as a sailor would say, from the particular district where he was born; but when away from home, all are Igbos. And yet considerable differences exist between different parts of this extensive country, and the dialects spoken also vary greatly. Those of which we heard during our voyage as being well marked are the Abo, Elugu, Isuama, and Aro, of which that Isuama is the most widely diffused, the safest, the best adapted for the lingua standard. Elugu is in the far north, close to Igara, and near to it, to the eastward, are two small districts, Isielu [hill-dwellers historically these parts of the Igbo-land are most hilly] and Isiago [Ishiagu]* (Eze et al., 1999:41,324, O.U. Kalu, 2002:351).

In all probability, Baikie had encountered at Idah and Idoma (Akpoto) a trader who told him of an "Elugu" (Enugu) town (the all-important Nike Market south of Nsukka which had acted as an *entrepot* for the exchange of goods and services between the north and the south at the time (Agaba, 2008:185). Nike, among some other Igbo towns, was at the time a major market center for the procurement of slaves and other trade goods (Afigbo, 1987:57-60).

What is, however, important to be underlined here is that this early contact with the northern Igbo country was short-lived and was only to be revived about fifty years later, following the pacification of Nigeria and subsequent establishment of colonial rule in the opening years of the twentieth century. Indeed, it has been argued that the conquest of the Nigerian communities and formal introduction of colonial rule prepared ground for the planting of Christian missionary influences. Thus, while environments such as the coastal towns and for the first time, outside Lagos, Abeokuta may have hankered after missionaries and were ready to erect buildings for teachers and pay the cost of educating their children (Ayandele, 1966:290). By the second half of the nineteenth century, Igboland waited for the opening years of the twentieth century. From this period onward, the collapse of the Aro Long Juju in about 1902 (which had provided a religious fulcrum for its numerous Igbo adherents) provided what E.A Ayandele describes as an insatiable desire for education in Igboland (Ayandele, 1966: 290-1). To better understand Ayandele's analysis, it may be apt to quote from his own bible:

> *Once the religious cohesion provided by the Long Juju had been demolished, the traditional intervillage and interclan warfare that had been the main feature of these atomized people was transformed into rivalry for the white man's education. Having tasted the military power of the white man most of all the Nigerian peoples, the village world collapsed much more quickly than the urban world of Yoruba. Thousands rushed into the village school where missions made acceptance of religious instruction the only condition for admission* (Ayandele, Ibid).

Continuing, Ayandele adds that

> *the desire of the Ibo (sic) for education compelled the society of the Holy Ghost Fathers to revolutionize its evangelistic strategy. The man who saw the necessity for doing this was Father*

(later Bishop) Shanahan. Hitherto Roman Catholic missions throughout the world had carried out their activities by the strategy of reductions or Christian villages. By this system slaves were purchased and settled around the priests, completely cut off from the rest of the community (Ayandele, Ibid).

The beneficiaries of the strategy mentioned in the foregoing statement were probably the Onitsha Igbo and their immediate neighbors. The reasons for this were obvious. For one, the River Niger, which flows through Onitsha, provided an enticing stimulus for large concentration of human settlements and commercial activities there (Okoye, 1996:136-137). Two, it was through the River that the missionaries such as Henry Venn, Samuel A. Crowther, J. C. Taylor, and Simon Jonas arrived at Onitsha to begin evangelical work. They built churches, schools, and hospitals at Onitsha and its environs toward the close of the nineteenth century and the opening years of the twentieth century (Okoye, 1996).We may recall the famous Niger Mission of 1857. It was Crowther who led the missionary arm of the mission.

On the other hand, the opening up of the Igbo hinterland for the so-called British "civilizing mission" had waited until the twentieth century. In Udi Division, to which Nkanu area, including Ugbawka (and Amauzam our study area), belong, its Christianization was preceded by series of military expeditions undertaken by the British in the opening years of the twentieth century. The aim was probably to humiliate the people to submit to the British suzerainty. F. K. Ekechi and E. A. Ayandele have respectively used the conquest theory to describe this phenomenon. According to them, the exactions of colonial rule played a principal role in the Igbo response to Christianity (Agbodike, 2008:111). To a large degree, the spirit of this theory might have defined the relationship between the Nkanu people and the British as between 1908 and 1914, detachments of the colonial military troops comprising few white officers and scores of African soldiers, carriers, and interpreters unleashed terrors on groups of Nkanu towns and villages. In these military exercises, towns like Akpugo, Nike, Amechi Idodo, Owo, Oruku, and their neighbors suffered some casualties in spite of their resistance to the invading British army (Afigbo, 1997:29; Mbah, 1997; Chukwu, 2008: 76-88).

In the subsequent years, Nkanu towns and villages, despite sustained resistance, suffered heavy casualties at the hands of the British troops. The heaviest (which gave rise to the use of Ugbawka as a refugee camp for other Nkanu indigenes fleeing from British attack) was the 1914 expedition which Akegbe-ugwu, supported by some other Nkanu clans, raised strong opposition against the British. In a reprisal that followed, the British organized attacks which resulted in the sacking of such Nkanu towns as Akpugo, Amurri, and Amagunze. However, other towns which were not immediately submerged by the deluge of British military expeditions provided ready haven for the invaded towns. And in this direction, Ugbawka was among the towns that were invaded by the British for receiving fleeing refugees from neighboring communities. According to F. P. Lynch, the Political Officer Number One Column for the British Administration, in a report:

> *It has been reported that some of the Amagunzes have taken refuge in the Ezza country. Many and varying reports come in that they are hiding in the fields of the surrounding towns such as Ihuopkara, Nara, Amechi (Idodo), Oborka (Ugboka/ Ugbawka), Oruku, Akporfu. The chiefs of these towns with the exception of Oborka have been in and stated they have driven away any who tried to come to the towns* (Afigbo, 1977; Chukwu, 2008).

It would probably appear from the foregoing account that the British military expeditions on the many Nkanu communities at the time would not only subdue (if only in relatively temporary term) whatever was the social crises among the communities but would also prepare the ground for the evangelization of the area beginning from the second decade of the twentieth century. Thus, from this decade, attempts were made to plant schools and churches in the communities.

THE CHURCH AND THE SCHOOL IN AMAUZAM

As pointed out in the preceding paragraphs after the traditional communities had been cowed into submission by the numerous military expeditions, the coast became calmer and clearer for the Christian missionaries to step in to build churches (Chukwu, 2007:83-84) and subsequently establish schools in the area. Even with their subjugation, the people still viewed with suspicion the coming of Christianity and Western education as made manifest in the church and the school. According to one informant, they still saw each as a subtle way of colonial suppression to which they must not succumb (Nwodo Edemba). But having resisted for so long, it would not take time before the people would succumb to the new wave of colonization (Enechukwu, 1993:314). The missionary agencies through which the Church and formal education were introduced into Nkanu land in the twentieth century were the Roman Catholic Mission (RCM) and the Primitive Methodist Missionary Society (PMMS) (Apenda, 2007:194). What perhaps would have been the third agency—the Church Missionary Society (CMS)—had confined its activities to the Enugu urban where it established the first primary school, Saint James School (CMS) now Colliery Primary School, Iva Valley, Enugu, in 1917 (Enechukwu, 1993:309).

In Nkanu land, the early Christian missionaries might have understood the psychology of the average Igbo person who, in the calculations of Taylor and Crowther, was emulative, moreso, when it had to do with book learning (Quoted in Enechukwu, 1993). Shanahan worked on this psychology, hence his thinking that,

> *If we go from town to town talking only about God, we know from experience that much of our effort brings no result. But no one is opposed to the schools* (Jordan, 1977:83).

Where perhaps in some Nkanu communities there was little or no opposition to the establishment of schools; in others, there was pronounced opposition. In Onicha Agu (Amagunze), in the 1930s, the teachers and the catechists were reportedly expelled from the community (Enechukwu, 1993:315). In Amauzam (Ugbawka), some male pupils of the Methodist School reportedly engaged one of their teachers, Mr. Nwigbo, on a physical combat in the 1960s (Nwodo, 2009). Mr. Nwigbo was said to be the youngest in the male-dominated school (Nwodo, 2009). These early oppositions notwithstanding, the Christian missionaries went ahead in their bid to establish primary schools in Nkanu communities.

Apart from the primary schools established at Amaigbo in Ozalla by the RCM in 1917 (which was followed in quick succession by the one established by the RCM at Nomeh in 1918, another at Ihuokpara by the RCM 1919), the Methodist Mission was to establish a school at Onicha Agu in 1920 (Enechukwu, 1993:311). In the next year (1921), the Primitive Methodist Church further beamed the light of formal education on Nkanu, when it established the Methodist Central School at Agbani and the Methodist School at Amauzam in the Obinagu Quarters of Ugbawka (Enechukwu, 1993:326).

It is believed that the arrangement for the establishment of a primary school at Amauzam traces its origin to an application by the Reverend A. Humphrey Richardson of the Primitive Methodist Church at Nara, a southern town in Nkanu. Entitled "Details of Application to Open a School at Obinagu" (Oboka), the application, dated March 1919, was directed to the District Officer (DO) in charge of Enugu Division. In the application, the Reverend Richardson conveyed the people's eagerness to have a school established in their village. This, he added, was demonstrable in their willingness to donate an acre of land for the school site (NAE/OP.198/19). The political leader of Ugbawka at the time was said to be Warrant Chief Aguoru Mba of the Umumba family in Amauzam. Consequently, the onus of mobilizing the family owners of the land in the village was said to have fallen on him (Edemba Nwobodoede). Having thus secured a rancour-free land through a donation by the community, it was now possible for the Methodist Missionary Society to establish a primary school at Amauzam in 1921(NAE/OP/198/19). The table below may help the reader to better understand when each primary school in Ugbawka was established and the missionary agency responsible for its founding:

Table one: Primary Schools in Ugbawka and Their Years of Establishment

S/N	Present name of School	Location	Year of founding	Former name	Proprietor
1.	Community Primary School	Amauzam	1921	Methodist School	Primitive Methodist Society (PMS)
2.	Community Primary School I	Isigwe	1927	Methodist School	,,
3.	Community Central School Amafor	Umuisu	1936	Methodist Group School	,,
4.	Community Primary School II	Isigwe	1936	St. James's School	Roman Catholic Mission (RCM)
5.	Primary School Ugbawka	Amafor	1952	St. Luke's Cath. School	,,
6.	Community Primary School	Amankwo	1952	St. Coleman's School	,,
7.	Community Primary School	Amagu	1953	St. Vincent's Catholic School.	,,
8.	Community Primary School	Obeagu	1957	Methodist School	PMS
9.	Comm. Primary School	Uhuona	1958	Methodist School	PMS
10.	Amaururu Primary School	Amaururu Uhuona	1965	St. Agnes's Catholic School	RCM

Source: Compiled by the author with some adaptation from Anayo Enechukwu (1993), *History of Nkanu* Enugu: Kauhof of Publishers, Chapter 14.

It is said that the first set of buildings for the Methodist School (now Community Primary School), Amauzam, were thatched mud houses. Among the pioneer pupils of the school were George Nwamba Nwuko, Jacob Nwamba Nwuko (Odawalu), Moses Nwodo Nwuko, Isaac Anyaji, and Chifu Nwa Chifu (Mbah, 1997:79). Others that later enrolled into the school included Emmanuel Mbah, Isaiah Nwamba Nwodo Nnamani,

Nwa-anya Nwuko Chifu Nwuko, and James Edemba (Nwodo Edemba, 2009). Apart from these ones who showed interest in educational matters, few others were inclined to spiritual affairs; hence, they became active members in the church school. For instance, Agbowo Eze Nwa Agbowo (jocularly called *Onye Isi Uka* because of the leading role he played in the church arm of the school) took on the name "Ephraim" at baptism, so did Nwolie Ogo Nwachifu Mba Chifu (the father of this author) when he took on the name "Timothy" at baptism. Ozo Edemba Nwodoede, who gave some of this information to the researcher, regretted that the death of his father in 1942 was responsible for his inability to go to school (Nwodoede, 2009).

It may be referred from the list of names given in the foregoing paragraph that no mention is made of a girl pupil of the school at the time. Perhaps, this could have had something to do with how much the society of the period perceived the womenfolk *vis-à-vis* education. In an interview with the author, Ozo Ezekiel Edemba noted that the society of the era did not see the girl-child as the specie meant for the white man's school. Rather, he added, the girl-child was meant for two things: early marriage and subjection to domestic and farmwork (Edemba, 2009). Normally, the catechist who doubled as the teacher also introduced side attractions such as the beating of percussion pots commonly called *Udu* and single-headed drums (*Samba*) to keep the young pupils and church members as a united family (Nwodo Edemba, 2009).

We may pause to ask, "What brand of education did the early missionary schools bring to the people?" Generally, the brand they brought to the people was encapsulated in the usual three *Rs*: arithmetic, writing, and reading. In respect of the last- mentioned point (reading), the pupils were taught metropolitan history and geography of Britain (Enechukwu, 1993:321). Apart from learning the basic Methodist doctrines and studying the Bible and religious texts written in Igbo, the early pupils were taught to read and write alphabets such as *A B C D* and *A B GB D* (Ifemesia, 1992:9). They were exposed to readings such as *Azundu-Ocha, Azundu-Oji, AlaBingo,* and *Omenuko*. The early pupils were also taught moral instruction as well as the importance of handicrafts (popularly called handiwork) (Ifemesia, 1992).

Besides, what appeared to have partly affected the morale and interest of the early pupils of the Amauzam School was the policy of grading the mission schools at the time (Ifemesia, 1992:16). This policy was applied to the school. From the beginning, says Sam Mbah, the grade of the Primitive Mission School at Amauzam was such that it did not offer beyond elementary one (Mbah, 1997:91). The implication of this was that many brilliant pupils from the village who ordinarily would have aspired to greater heights educationally got stuck at primary one. This ugly trend continued until 1936 when the Methodist Group School at the Umuisu village, Ugbawka, came on the stream to offer elevated opportunities for determined pupils (Mbah, 1997). But at that time, how many pupils from Amauzam were willing and courageous enough to cover the distances to acquire the *Golden Fleece* at Umuisi? The reason for this was obvious. Since the 1930s witnessed spates of fear and uncertainty which appeared to have pervaded the length and breadth of the Ugbawka, following the 1923 civil strife (NAE/MILGOV.13/1/15) between the *Obia* and *Amadi*, in parts of Nkanu, it was pretty difficult for average parents to allow their children to travel long distances to attend schools far away from their immediate community for fear of being abducted (Nwodo Edemba).

WHY WAS AMAUZAM THE FIRST TO RECEIVE THE LIGHT OF EDUCATION IN UGBAWKA?

The question as to why Amauzam was the first village to receive the light of Western education in Ugbawka has generated debate in both informed and uninformed circles. This research may not go the whole hog in reeling out the opinions for and against this line of thought. But we may concern ourselves with two principal factors which might have accounted for the successful introduction of the church and formal education in Amauzam first before other villages in Ugbawka. They were stable political leadership in the village and proximity to Agbani, a rail station town in central Nkanu land.

In respect of stable political leadership, the thinking in certain quarters is that Amauzam as a community was better endued with leaders of sound minds and a sense of direction at the time. Apart from Aguoru Mba of the Umumba kindred, and who at the time was the warrant chief of Ugbawka, other kindreds (*Umunna*) were said to be avowedly committed to the Amauzam project (Nwodo Edemba). As noted earlier in this paper, this commitment was made manifest in the rancour-free manner in which the community donated the land on which the school was built. This was also the case with the land on which the teachers' houses were built. It was the same thing that applied in respect of the land on which the school's football pitch was erected, when for instance the Edemba Nwatu family of the Umumba kindred donated their parcels of land to the school authority for this purpose (Edemba, 2009). Reverend Richardson, who applied for the establishment of the school at Amanzam in 1919, had noted among other things, that there was no dispute whatever about the ownership of the school land (NAE/OP198/19).

To better understand the factor of proximity to Agbani, we may recall that at the start of the European Christian missionary enterprise in Eastern Nigeria, the major missionary agencies carved the region into areas of influence to reduce undue tension and rivalry among themselves (NAE/OP198/19). For instance, while the Church Missionary Society (CMS) and the Roman Catholic Mission (RCM) took over the evangelization of the Niger-Awka-Udi-Enugu axis following their earlier activities in Onitsha at the beginning of the twentieth century, the Presbyterian Mission concentrated their missionary activities on the Cross River and its environs, including the Cross River Igbo areas of Arochukwu, Ohafia, and so forth. On their part, the Methodists took over the evangelization of the major towns and cities where the railway stations were located and their environs (NAE/OP198/19). Ekechi has argued that the Methodists seriously attempted to expand their sphere of influence from Uzuakoli northward (Ekechi, 1972:142). They anxiously eyed Okigwe as an important center from which to evangelize the neighboring towns (Ekechi, 1972). This policy of rail evangelism might have coincided with the construction of the Eastern lines of the Nigerian Railway from Port Harcourt to Enugu in 1916 (Chukwu, 2008:88). With the numerous stations that dotted the rail lines, the Methodists were able to plant their branch churches and establish schools at the station towns and environs. Thus, the coming of the Agbani railway station held out a number of fortunes, which included the planting of churches and schools in the neighboring towns and villages. In other words, with the rail station at Agbani, coupled with the Central Methodist School there and the enterprising missionary activities, it was not long before Amauzam, a village that shares land borders with Agbani, would be reached by the Methodists (NAE/OP198/19).

FACTORS THAT DISCOURAGED CONTINUED MANPOWER DEVELOPMENT AT THE EARLY STAGE

In the previous section of this paper, we examined the steps taken by the European colonialists of various ranks in their attempt to penetrate the Nigerian space, especially the Igbo country. We were particular about their expansionist endeavor in Amauzam, pointing out when and how the Methodist School Amauzam came in 1921, as well as the people's initial reaction to the development. The preceding section of the paper also considered the factors that influenced the choice of Amauzam for the Church and School. Considering the early head start which Amauzam had, searching questions have been asked as to why there was to be a nosedive by the community in terms of manpower development. Clearly put, the thinking is that the community should have, over the years, produce generations of quality leaders in diverse areas of human endeavor. Alas, this has not been so due partly to a slide in manpower development. Let us, therefore, consider some possible factors that may have contributed to this state of affairs. Below are some of the factors.

Marriage to traditional agriculture. Over the years, scholars and commentators have advanced as a reason abundance of rich arable land in Nkanu as one of the factors that made the people, unlike their *Agbaja* counterparts, latecomers to the colonial civil service as well as recruitment into the Enugu coalfields (Chukwu, 2008:85). This was notwithstanding their proximity to Enugu urban. In a study, PEH Hair describes Nike (and possibly other Nkanu communities) as showing a disdain to work on the coalfields because they "had plenty of land" (Hair n.d.). To a great extent, the argument about the abundance of rich arable land in Nkanu remains a truism. But what is contestable is that every Nkanu man was vocationally engaged in farmwork. While in the past Amauzam people possessed a large expanse of land in parts of Ugbawka, the real tilling of the farmland was carried out by their retinue of domestic servants. To this end, it would only be unfair to the people's conscience to continue to band the argument that their marriage to traditional agriculture cut them off from acquiring formal education when others were scampering for it.

Social lifestyle. Because in the past Amauzam people had engaged the services of domestic laborers (in large numbers) who served them faithfully, they were to find it difficult to abandon this old way of life for the new. On the other hand, the former servants saw Christianity and the new school system as providing them with social security and cultural emancipation from the clutches of enslavement. In the circumstance, the ex-servants embraced the duo of Christianity and education tenaciously.

Policy of grading the early schools. The policy whereby the early schools were graded by the missionary proprietors might have discouraged pupils from aspiring to greater heights on the educational ladder. In the 1920s, 1930s, 1940s, and 1950s, when a state of uncertainty pervaded Ugbawka town, parents, for fear of abduction, were discouraged from sending their children to schools in the neighboring villages. In the same vein, if the Methodist School at Amauzam were to have been allowed to operate up to at least Standard IV or so, the pioneer pupils would have graduated to attend the Methodist College at Uzuakoli or other colleges in Eastern Nigeria (Philip Chukwu, 2005).

Government attitude toward secondary education in Nkanu land. Studies have shown that the colonial government and even the missionary agencies maintained a lukewarm attitude toward the establishment of colleges in this area. It is to be observed that it was only on the eve of Nigeria's independence in the 1950s that the Methodists managed to establish a teacher-training college at Umueze, Awkunanaw, while the same Methodists had earlier founded colleges at Uzuakoli, Ihube, and Ovim, etc. The Catholics that had invaded Nkanu area would not on their fit deem to establish any colleges in the area as they had previously done in the Onitsha and Owerri areas. In fact, the first secondary school in Nkanu land—the Boys Secondary School Umueze, Awkunanaw,—began academic activities in 1972. In 1976, the Boys Secondary School, Nara, began academic activities, whereas Ugbawka, a town with a total number of ten primary schools established by both the PMS and the RCM before the outbreak of the Nigerian Civil War in 1967, would only establish a secondary through a community effort in 1981. While recommending that the reader may study Table 2 below, it may, however, be necessary to underline the fact that the Christian missionary agencies did not encourage the growth of secondary school education in Nkanu clan.

Table 2

Post primary schools in the traditional Nkanu Clan and the years of their founding

1.	Boys Secondary School, Umueze, Awkunanaw	-	1972
2.	Boys Secondary School, Nara	-	1976
3.	Girls Secondary School, Amuri	-	1977
4.	Boys High School, Ozalla	-	1977
5.	Community Secondary School, Amagunze	-	1978
6.	Girls Secondary School, Obe	-	1979
7.	Boys Comprehensive Secondary School, Akpugo	-	1980
8.	Boys Secondary School, Akpugo	-	1980
9.	Unateze Girls Secondary School, Nara	-	1980
10.	Boys Secondary School, Obe	-	1981
11.	Community Secondary School, Ugbawka	-	1981
12.	Girls Secondary School, Akegbe-ugwu	-	1982
13.	Community Secondary School, Nomeh	-	1982
14.	Community Secondary School, Ihuokpara	-	1982
15.	Community Secondary School, Nkerefi	-	1983
16.	Community Secondary School, Obinagu Akpugo	-	1983
17.	Community Secondary School, Owo	-	1983
18.	Community Secondary School, Agbani	-	1983

Source: Enechukwu, *History of Nkanu* p. 335

How to Mobilize for Formal Education

Mobilizing for formal education may not be easy; it may sometimes be painful since often, the results of such investments are not immediate. Often, it requires patience and perseverance on the part of the investor to nurture the seed of educational investment, for at harvest, not only he/she but also the family, the community, and the entire society stand to reap the benefits. To therefore share in these bounties, the following rules must be observed:

Involvement of parents: Parents, no matter how low or high their income may be, should see the education of their children as a priority. Until the 1970s, when government took over schools from the mission, parents were known to have privately sponsored their children and wards through the school system.

Award of scholarships: Often, when the issue of scholarships is raised, our minds quickly race to government-sponsored scholarship schemes. But beyond government scholarships, individuals, groups, and corporate bodies should have a stake in building the society's future manpower through scholarship schemes.

Community efforts: This researcher is of the opinion that communities, including Amauzam, should have a common pool to which each adult member of the community should contribute either on quarterly or yearly basis. The common pool will enable the indigent but brilliant pupils/students to be sponsored up to the university level.

Involvement of town unions: The implementation of the back-to-school call may not be easy. But to make the burden lighter, all hands must be on deck. These hands may include all the members of the community, including groups, the town union, market women, and religious organizations. The history of the African-Americans' emancipation in the U.S. is replete with the giant strides made by two denominational institutions and black literary societies founded to encourage higher education in Pennsylvania and Ohio. The denominations included the Presbyterian Church, under whose sponsorship the Lincoln University, Pennsylvania, was incorporated in 1854. Eminent African leaders, such as Nnamdi Azikiwe, were known to have been educated at Lincoln. Of significance is that the education of black Africans made significant contributions in the abolitionist process in the USA and the independence movements in Africa (Chukwu, 2007:8-12). If, therefore, we should make progress in education and in all other areas of life, all groups in our society should be involved in the educational process.

CONCLUSION

A lot of issues have been raised in this paper. The paper has deliberately deemphasized the expected role of governments in assisting communities educationally. Of course, the researcher is aware that governments do assist communities that have embarked on projects aimed at developing their people educationally. The argument has often been that children abandon education for trading and early childhood marriages. This is one side of the story. Parents, guardians, relations, and communities should on their part provide the enabling environment for the growth of formal education, if the future will be assured.

Besides, Nigerian governments should provide congenial atmosphere to make education process in the country attractive. Going by the trends of events in the country, our governments can only be seen to be paying lip service to the provision of education. At present in parts of the country, there appears to be an astronomical rise in the growth of private schools, most of which charge high fees. And how many average Nigerian parents can send their children to such schools? Regrettably, too, public schools are poorly funded by the governments. It has been observed that strikes by teachers at all levels of our educational institutions are now a yearly ritual. The common reason for this has often been traced to either no-salary situation or underfunding of the school system. Governments are, therefore, called upon to take the issue of adequate funding of the schools seriously. If perhaps yesterday failed us, today should not be allowed to slip out of our hands.

REFERENCES

Afigbo, A. E. (1977), "The Pangs of Social Adjustment among the Nkanu Igbo, the First Phase, 1907-1924." A paper presented at the 22nd Annual Congress of the Historical Society of Nigeria at the University of Benin, Benin City, 27-31 March, p. 29.

- The Igbo and Their Neighbors: Intergroup Relations in Southeastern Nigeria to 1953. Ibadan: University Press Ltd., 1987.

Agaba, John Ebute (2008), "The Nigerian Civil War and the Changing Migration Patterns of the Igbo into Idoma-land: 1967-2007," in Armstrong M. Adejo (ed.) *The Nigerian Civil War Forty Years After: What Lesson?* Makurdi: Aboki Publishers.

Agbodike, C.C (2008), A Centenary of Catholic Missionary Activities in Ihiala 1908-2009. Nkpor: Globe Communications.

Apenda, Anthony Z (2007), *The Imperative of Historical Sources in the Reconstruction of African Traditional Religion* in Mike O. Odey et al., (eds) Historical Research and Methodology in Africa. Makurdi: Aboki Publishers.

Ayandele, E. A. (1966), *The Missionary Impact on Modern Nigeria* 1842-1914: A Political and Social Analysis London: Longman Group Ltd.

Chukwu, Philip (68), An Oral interview at Amanfu (Ugbawka), 26/12/2005.

Chukwu, Dan O. (2004), "Abyssinia Nwafor Orizu and the Philosophy of African Irredentism" in G. O. Ozumba (ed.) A Colloquium on African Philosophy Calabar: Jochrisam Publishers (2007)

- (2007), An Introduction to Nigerian Political History, 3rd Ed. Enugu: Glory Publication.
- (2008), "Eastern Nigerian and the British War Machines: Select Case Studies" AAU: African Studies Review.

- (2008), "Coal and the Rise of the City of Enugu, 1909-2008" in Onwuka, Njoku, and Obi Iwuagwu (eds) Topics in Igbo Economic History. Lagos: First Academic Publishers.
- (2007/2008), "Background to the Era of New Abolitionism" Journal of the Historical Society of Nigeria Vol.17.

Edemba, Chris A. Being the product of an interview at Amauzam, 22/11/2009.

Edemba, E. N. (80), An oral interview at Amauzam, 19/12/09

Edemba, Nwodo (70). An interview at Amauzam, 19/12/09

Ekechi, F. K. (1972), Missionary Enterprise and Rivalry in Igboland 1857-1914. London: Frank Case and Co. Ltd.

Enechukwu, A. (1993), History of Nkanu, Enugu: Kaufhof Publishers.

Eze, Dons, et al., (1994), *The WAWA Struggle: A History of Factional Dissension in Iboland,* Enugu: Delta Publication Ltd.

Hair, P. E. H. "Unpublished Report on Enugu" (nd).

Harbison, F. and Meyers, C. A. (1964), *Education, Manpower Development, and Economic Growth: Strategies of Human Resources.* New York: McGrow Hill.

Ifemesie, C. (1992), Anglican Centenary, 1892-1992 An Outline History.

Kalu, O. U. *Igbo Traditional Religious Systems* in Ofomata, G. E. K. (ed.) A Survey of the Igbo Nation. Onitsha: Africana First Publishers Limited, 2002.

Mbah, Sam (1997), *A History of Ugbawka: From Precolonial Times to Present.*

Enugu: Reynolds Publishers.

Mead, Margaret (1943) "Our Educational Emphasis in Primitive Perspective" American Journal of Sociology vol. 48.

NAE/OP/198/19 (1919), "Primitive Methodist Missionary Society: Applications for Permission to Open Schools in Enugu Division"

NAE/MILGOV 13/1/15 (1936) "Intelligence Report on Amurri-Ugbawka Group in Udi Division." Nwachuku, Daisy N. (ed.) (1990) Contemporary Issues in Nigerian Education and

Development: Structures, Principles, Analysis, and Solutions for the Twenty-First Century. Enugu: Gospel Communications International Ltd.

Nwodo, Sunday (63+). An oral interview with the researcher at Amauzam 14/11/09.

Okafor, Richard C. (2004), "Nigeria Organology and Classification of African Musical Instruments" in R. C. Okafor and L. N. Emeka (ed.) Nigerian Peoples and Culture. 4th ed. Enugu: New Generation Books.

Okoye, T. O. (1996), The City in Southeast Nigeria Onitsha: University Publishing Company.

Oladesu, E. and Yishau, O. (2010), "Cabinet: The Worst Case Scenarios." The Nation Newspaper. Saturday, March 20

Orizu, A. A. N. (1994), Liberty or Chains Africa Must Be Nnewi: Horizontal Publishers. Stroud, James B. (1940), Psychology of Education New York Longman, Green and Co.

Todaro, M. P. and Smith, S. C. (2003), Economic Development 8th Edition Delhi; Pearson Education, Inc.

An All-Inclusive Shared Governance Model that Is Transparent and Enhances Trust, Understanding, and Unity between the Faculty and the Administration

Ghyasuddin Ahmed, Ph.D.
Virginia State University

ABSTRACT

Recent studies on shared governance provide mixed messages—some positive, some negative, and some neutral views on effective and smooth functioning of the system. He realized that the current negativity is coming from a type of "dual" decision-making process in our shared government system that can easily be made a single, extremely efficient, smooth, and transparent. Based on author's long and personal involvement and experiences in two cultures, he conceptualized this model that should address most of the concerns and questions raised on the current functioning of the shared governance system in the USA. It is a three-tier and a two-way—mostly bottom-up and top-down decision-making body. Most current structure, on the other hand, is somewhat disjointed as faculty and administrators decide separately, and the administration can turned down the faculty decisions. The current faculty senate structure almost totally neglects the key decision makers—the president, the vice presidents, the deans/directors, and the chairs as none of them are members. Under the proposed system, both the management team and the faculty take joint decisions on all academic, as well as personnel matters, for academic staff and all academic decision making for the students. The three tiers are: (1) the department; (2) the school;

and (3) the senate. At the department and school levels, the entire faculty and the administration are involved in the shared governance structure.

They are named as Departmental and School Boards. At the top level is the faculty senate that is mainly composed of senior faculty and the president and the provost from the administration as members. Registrar's office senior staff provides secretarial services to this committee—they remain as facilitators and resource persons on rules and regulations but cannot vote for any decision. Because the top administration and the faculty take joint decisions together, the decision making is fast, and administration has no scope of turning down the faculty senate's decisions because they are jointly involved. This brings greater harmony, peace, and tranquility between the two major players of academic decision makers. However, the highest decision-making body—the Board of Trust—or any other similar organ has the right to accept or reject any decision taken by any other lower entity; but usually, it does not interfere in most academic matters.

For personnel decisions, after the department takes its decision, that is sent to the school level appointment, promotion and tenure committee that is chaired by the academic provost. Each school has its own committee with the senior academics of all the departments of the school and the dean as the members. If the chair of the department is below the associate professor level, he/she only attends that part of the meeting that discusses candidates from the department. The personnel decision of this committee is then forwarded to the University Board of Trust or Visitors for final decision. If this committee finds any issue doubtful or wants further clarification on a candidate, that particular case is sent back to the school/department committee.

Keywords: ideal share governance; all-inclusive governance structure; school boards; high-powered appointment, promotion, and tenure committee; and school and faculty senate secretariats.

INTRODUCTION

Delays in decision making, dismay, distrust, disunity, lack of respect, lack of transparency, rifts of different magnitude, and tensions between the faculty and the administration are most common problems observed in recent studies on shared governance in our educational institutions (Arenson, 1997; Benjamin and Carroll, 1996; Baldridge, ed. 1971; Bing, and Dye, 1996; Birnbaum, 1989; Clark, 1997; Cowley, 1980; Epstein, 1974; Finn Jr. and Manno, 1996; Gilmour Jr. 1991; Healy, 1995, 1996, and 1997; Hines and Hartmark, 1980; Heyman, 1997; Hines and Hartmark, 1980; Hodgkinson, 1968; Ingram, 1993; Kauffman, 1980; Keeton, 1977; Keohane, 1996; Kerr, 1994; Lazerson, 1997; Leslie, 1996; Letherman, 1998; Lewis, 1993; MacTaggart and Associates, 1996; Magner, 1997; McConnell, 1970; Miles et al., 1997; Michaelson, 1998; Miller et al., 1996; Miller and Kang, 1999; Newman, 1987; Newquist, 1998; Novak, 1996; Nussbaum, 1998; Perley, 1997; Pettit and Kirkpatrick, 1984; Ridgely, 1993; Riley and Baldridge, 1977; Ruppert, 1994; Schuster, 1991; Scott, 1997; Saint John, 1995; Trani, 1997; Wallenfeldt, 1983; Wolvin, 1991). Some presidents of institutions of higher learning complain that shared governance requires "extensive consultation with different entities that interferes with the administrator's ability to do their jobs properly" (Healy, 1997). Unilateral decision is always quick, and it takes very little time to decide, but the involvement of other people is an essential part of all democratic process, and democracy is always be time consuming. On another negative note Miller et al., (1996 and 98) reported that several legal decisions have greatly limited the legal rights of faculty to be involved in shared governance system.

On positive notes, Miller et al. (1996 and 98) concluded that the administrators become "conduits" for decision making and planning activities in *that the faculty are listened to, trusted and respected for their involvement and contributions.* Another study (Miller 1999) reported that the *faculty members are increasingly called upon to accept the roles as decision and policy makers in the institutional governance activities.* He further observed that *they (faculty) often serve at the will of senior administrators* and suggested that *the faculty governance body must work to establish ground rules for their involvement.* Miller and McCormack (2004) investigated the shared governance in higher education and found that it (shared governance) has formed deep roots in institutional functioning and behavior. Results also indicated that the faculty members, who have a research focus, generally are not awarded responsibility, but they (Miller and McCormack) believe that *senior faculty must be involved in curriculum design and graduation requirements.* Miller and Miller (1997) observed that professional education, colleges, and universities have taken leadership roles in defining many of the current trends and issues facing the higher education institutions. Utilizing a leading professional college as a case study, data indicated some dissatisfaction with reward structures and *a call for greater faculty empowerment in policy decisions.*

Millette (2004) provided an overview of academics and governance at historically black colleges and universities (HBCUs). He started with a narration of his own school's shared governance status, the problems that he observed and then studied some other HBCUs. His observations are similar to those reported above, i.e., *conflicts and cold wars are the norms of shared governance system that resulted in some major changes in the top administration, but in spite of such changes the ill feelings and rifts between the two major players still remain.*

The American Federation of Teachers (AFT) listed six principles of shared governance that envision the achievement of: (1) high academic standards; (2) academic freedom; (3) primacy in decisions on academic personnel and status; (4) the participation in shared governance; (5) significant roles for all in the shared governance structure; and (6) support of shared governance in the accrediting agencies' standards. The AFT expects a complementary rather than competitive function between the union and the *governance bodies.*

This review shows both positive and negative aspects of current shared governance structures being practiced in U.S. institutions of higher learning. In sum, these findings suggest that the shared governance system is working better in one and worse in other institutions. A number of factors may be responsible for this. First, the key actors—the administration—and faculty's attitude, ego, perceptions, personality, and experience with one another is a key factor. Second, the disagreements between the administrators and some leading faculty may create souring relationships between the two key players. Third, personal interests of key players take precedence over the organizational interests, creating conflicts between the two forces. Fourth, shared governance structures are also responsible for creating both positive and negative experiences in the system.

While working for a new faculty senate constitution, I have realized that our governance system is not "ideally" shared and started thinking critically based on my personal involvements and experiences in two societies. I thought of the ways to meet the ATF's goals of achieving the set principles effectively and efficiently and have come up with an ideal "all-inclusive system" in which the faculty, the administration, and the students take decisions jointly on all academic issues. Such an ideal system, I believe, is needed more when most service providers (the faculty and the administrators) are not only highly educated and skilled but also highly argumentative, egoistic, energetic, judgmental, and sensitive. As will be seen, this suggested model is complementary and not competitive that fulfills the AFT expectations.

Problems identified in these reviews and my nearly two decades of personal involvements in faculty senates and academic management processes led me to come up with a model that *I believe will resolve or greatly diminish most of the problems of current shared governance structures as reported in many studies referred above.* We need to change our culture of shared governance from a "union-oriented" to an "all-inclusive governance system" that will make governance structure truly "shared." The current union-oriented system is not totally shared in that the two groups—the administrators and the faculty—tend to decide matters independent of each other, and the administration is not bound to accept the faculty's decisions. I consider this separate decision-making process to be the main sources of problems that have been presented in the introduction above. Academic and management decisions certainly need the involvement of all those who work in these settings—especially when most service providers are not only highly educated and skilled but are also highly critical, egoistic, energetic, judgmental, moral, and sensitive. Taking joint decisions, therefore, will help achieve the six principles of shared governance envisioned by the AFT—it will surely complement rather than compete the interests of the two groups of highly respected professionals in our educational system. In other words, the joint decision-making process is likely to bring more harmony, peace, transparency, trust, and unity among all key players of the academic institutions of higher learning.

In the next section, I have suggested an all-encompassing shared governance system that I consider as an "ideal model." The proposed structure will make, I believe, the achievement of institutional objectives smooth, timely, and resource efficient, provided that we can accept a new culture of nonunionized shared governance structure. Unionism may be unnecessary when it comes to achieving of common personnel goals of the two involved but ideologically envious parties. Personnel decisions may also be taken involving the two major groups—the administrators and the faculty—as is also envisioned and discussed in this paper.

An All-Inclusive Shared Governance System: An Ideal Model. I call this proposed shared governance structure as "ideal" because idealism is important to make any system or process work efficiently and equitably. At times, however, idealism fails because of two reasons: (a) actors' rejection of the process or actors have different interests or ideas and (b) the structure is complicated or complex. Weber's ideal bureaucratic model is working throughout the world, even though some rules are bended here and there by some actors. In other words, no ideal system works 100 percent ideally, but any system having no ideals or when ideals fail to account for actors' individual rather than group needs and benefits, that type of idealism is likely to fail. Human desire, ego, greed, needs, and temptations (all fall under interest) are the sources that make idealisms fail.

Figure 1 shows the ideal, nonunionized, and all-inclusive three-tier shared governance system that has the active representation and participation of all faculty, administration, and student representatives at all levels. In this model, the shared governance system is constituted through statues or through a built-in legal structure. *In this regime, there is no need for any (faculty senate) constitution as all aspects of the academic and management system are clearly mandated in the statutes or legally incorporated rules and regulations in the overall management system of the institution. Compositions, rules, and regulations are clearly specified in the statutes for smooth and efficient functioning of the institution.* In this system, the faculty is spared of the laborious, at times complicated, process of holding elections every year and at times from "begging" people to run for key offices of the disjointed shared governance structure and its committees. In this proposed system, by virtue of their positions, each and every official of the university are directly and indirectly involved in the shared decision-making process that is outlined in Figure 1 and discussed below.

It is usually a bottom-up approach that is truly shared in every sense of the term, but it may also be top-down meaning that top administrators' ideas are passed on to the senate for review and decisions. The process has three levels: (1) the department at the bottom; (2) the schools in the middle; and (3) the university-wide senate at the top of academic decision-making process.

For all the three sectors of the institution, there is the University Council consisting of members from: (1) the faculty senate; (2) the staff senate, and (3) the student government association (SGA). All common issues for these three entities are dealt by the University Council. It should be a relatively small body—representing senior officials of all the three bodies—the faculty, the staff, and the SGA. The focus for this paper, however, is the sharing of academic and management decisions for the faculty in the governance structure of the institution of higher learning representing all the major players.

1. *The Departmental Boards*

At the department and school levels, all academic and management staffs (chairs and deans/directors) are required to participate in a democratic decision-making process that is truly shared. But when it comes to the highest decision-making level, beyond the school, it is mostly the senior officials—both faculty and administration that take decisions together. The faculty senate activities are directly linked with the department as all faculty and staff are required to participate in almost all academic and management decision-making activities of the respective department. The departmental board monthly meeting minutes are sent to the school board, and school boards' minutes are sent to faculty senate. This way, the activities of all entities become public, and other departments and schools know what is going on around the campus. Any member at each level of this shared government system may raise questions and concerns on any issue from those minutes. The chair of the department remains as the "captain of the ship" or the leader and the facilitator. He/she can take emergency decisions that must be ratified by the full body when it meets.

Faculty and chair appointments or personnel requirements, sabbatical leave, or any other personnel matter are also discussed and decided by the whole department in accordance with the needs of its program. Annual review, tenure, and promotion cases are initiated by the individual faculty in consultation with the chair, and then it is submitted to the dean for placement at the school level Appointment, Promotion, and Tenure Committee for decision, as discussed under the School Board section. *This committee is outside the domain of the academic decision-making process or the senate, as discussed later.* At times, these personnel decisions may also be made by a designated small committee if the department wants to handle that way.

All decisions are approved by the whole department. The affected members of the staff excuse themselves for that part of the meetings that discuss their individual personnel issues and problems. At the beginning of each academic year, a junior faculty member may be elected to act as the Secretary of the Departmental Boards. This person is responsible to take the minutes of the meetings, or it may be done by the departmental secretary if the person is competent enough to do so. Minutes are distributed to all staff as soon as possible so that each member take his/ her follow-up activities and report back to the next meeting. *As has been stated before, a copy of the minutes is also sent to the school board secretariat that becomes a part of relevant document for the school board meetings.* From the student body, at least one student, majoring in the discipline, is elected or selected by the SGA each academic year from among the students of the department. When more than one discipline is represented in one department, at least one student from each discipline represents the departmental boards.

Figure 1: An All-Inclusive Three-Tire Bottom-Up and Top-Down Shared Governance System

International Journal for Social Science Research and Practice (IJSSRP) Volume 1 Nos. 1 & 2 December 2012

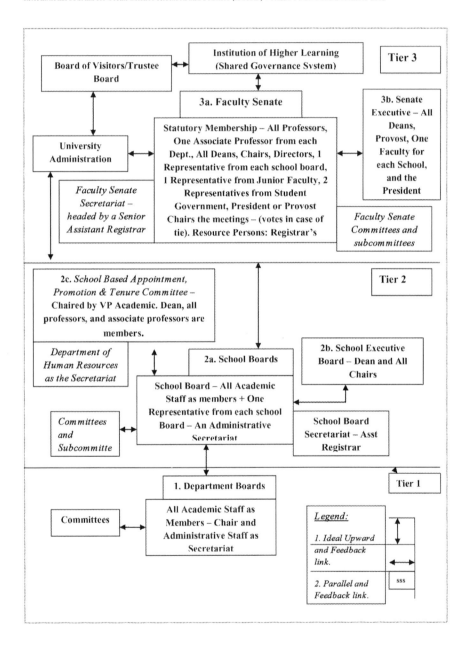

2. The School Boards

The school boards, as far as the faculty senate is concerned, have two entities: (a) the general body; and (b) the executive boards as described below. The respective dean/director of each school is the chief of the school board. *At the school level, a high powered committee (2c), not a part of the school board, may also be constituted to handle the personnel/human resources matters that deals with appointment, promotion, and tenure or any other personnel issue of academic staff.* These are discussed below.

2a. The General School Board

As has been stated before, the faculty board is composed of all academic staff of the school, all chairs, the dean/director, one representative from each other school, and a senate representative are members. It also takes at least two students of the school that are selected by the SGA each year. Each school board is supported by an assistant registrar and her/his support staff that is based in dean's/director's office. The assistant registrar is responsible for all managerial activities including taking the minutes of each school and executive board meetings. School board's meeting minutes are distributed along with the agenda of the meeting well in advance so that all members can go through those for their respective actions and prepare themselves to participate in the ensuing meeting. Attendance of the meetings is mandatory for each and every member. Anyone unable to attend the meeting is expected to submit a letter of apology to the secretariat, with reasons for the absence. Each minute of the meeting publishes a list of all members in three categories: (1) members present; (2) members absent with apologies; and (3) members absent without apology. Faculty having classes during the meeting time may be absent with apology, or students may be given library or other academic works so that the faculty can attend the meetings. Different school boards and faculty senate meet at different dates so that the school board representative of other schools can attend both school boards and the senate meetings. Meetings are usually scheduled in the afternoon from 2:00 p.m. Depending on the volume of decisions to be taken, the meetings can, however, also be held from morning and may continue throughout the day, with lunch break.

2b. The School Board Executive

The composition of the school board executive is the dean/director of the respective school and all chairs under the school. They meet before the general meetings of the school board and the senate meetings to discuss issues and to make sure that each and every issue of the school is in order. Executives take strategies to defend their programs or issues to be raised and discussed for decision before each school board/senate meetings. This body (School Board Executive) also can take emergency decisions when the school board is not in session. Any such decision, however, has to be ratified by the board in the next meeting after the executive decision has been taken. The school board secretariat is also a part of this executive body and does all secretarial works for the two boards. All records, related to the school board and executive, remain in the office of the secretariat located in each school under the supervision of the dean/director. Each school has its own secretariat and other support staff needed to run the activity of the school boards efficiently.

2c. School Appointment, Promotion, and Tenure Committee (independent from the "Academic" Senate)

This is an independent entity from the school boards and the faculty senate and is composed of all professors and associate professors of the school and chaired by the vice president of academic affairs. The dean of the school is also required to be present in this meeting. *There is no student representation in this committee.* Its job is to consider, review, and recommend candidates for appointment, promotion, retention, and tenure that have been approved by each department. If the chair of any department is below the rank of associate professor, he/she attends this personnel management meeting only for the part that discusses that department's candidates. Any member whose case is discussed in this meeting must recuse from that part of the meeting.

Contrary to the school board, the secretariat for this committee is the human resources department of the university. The school secretariat, however, does all the preparation works for each and every case of the school and also attends this "personnel" committee. During the A&PC meeting, the human resource department becomes secretariat of the committee and takes minutes of all discussion and decisions both at the school and university levels meetings. At the school level, the departmental board's decision is thoroughly examined, scrutinized, and decision taken by the school appointment, promotion, and tenure committee, irrespective of the recommendations from the department. In other words, this personnel committee is not a rubber stamp of the departmental recommendations. This committee may accept, reject, change, or seek clarification or additional information on any candidate or issue before taking any decision related to each and every case from the department. This situation makes the department to work very thoroughly so that its recommendations are fair and equitable that usually leads the school committee to mostly accept the recommendations from the department after a thorough scrutiny. This committee meets at least once during each academic term. The decision of this committee is then forwarded to the Board of Visitors (BoV) or the Trustee Board, whatever may be the name of the highest decision-making body, for final decision. If any candidate is not satisfied with promotion, tenure, or any other personnel decision of the school level committee the, affected persons may make an appeal to the Board of Trustee or Board of Visitor or the highest decision-making body. Trustee Board or Board of Visitor's decision is final.

Because the provost is directly involved in the decision process along with the faculty, all cases directly go to the highest body—the Board of Trustee or the BoV. This process saves time, by one stage, and enhances the positive relationship between the administration and the faculty. During the meeting, the chair (VP) usually does not try to influence the decision unless there is a tie. He/she may, however, argues and provides examples from past cases/issues and her/his thoughts to convince the committee. The faculty may provide counter arguments, thoughts, and examples without making it a conflict issue. People may have disagreement on any issue, but that does not make them enemy. Disagreement and healthy argument/criticism is the best strength of democratic process that must be accepted, honored, and followed to make the democratic process work better.

3. *The University (Faculty) Senate*

The highest academic decision-making body is the University (Faculty) Senate. At the senate levels, all professors (and all associate professors, when there are few professors in position), the department chairs, directors, deans of schools, *the president, the vice president of academic affairs*, two representative from each school (elected/selected during the first meeting, usually at the beginning of the academic year), two representatives from junior faculty (assistant professors and below) of each school compose the membership of the Senate. The president or the vice president of academic affairs, in the absence of the president, chairs all meetings. There is a built-in faculty *senate secretariat system that is managed by a unit of the registrar's office and is headed by a senior assistant registrar who is supported by a couple of assistants from the same department, i.e., the registrar's office.* The above process is a departure from the current union type system in which a chair of the senate is elected from among the faculty who preside over all meetings of the senate. The faculty may not be willing to give up this role under the modified system, but considering the advantages of taking joint decisions and faculty having the ultimate decision maker and the administration agreeing on all decisions taken in the senate, rifts and tensions between the administration and the faculty are eliminated/reduced. This way, decision-making process becomes more transparent, and administration cannot change the decision because that has been taken jointly.

Other senior personnel from the registrar's office, including the Registrar, the deputy, and the assistant registrars also attend the senate meetings regularly, but they do not participate in the decision-making process—they only remain as resource persons to provide information that might be needed with regard to rules and regulations pertaining to academic or other related legal issues. Neither the officers from registrar's office nor the presiding officer vote. The vice president, if not presiding, votes. However, if there is a tie, the presiding officer (the president) also votes. *The president usually conducts the meetings while the vice president of academic affairs attends each and every senate meeting along with other administration personnel, as specified above. The senate meets between two to three times during a semester as per the schedules usually set well in advance of the academic year and approved by the senate. The secretarial is responsible for planning and preparing the various activities, including the schedules, preparing and distributing the minutes, keeping all records of the senate, and do any other duties given by the senate and its committees.*

Schedules are published in the university calendar/catalogue so that all involved parties can make plans right from the beginning of the academic year to attend these meetings that are binding to its members. Minutes of the meetings and agenda are distributed by this secretariat well in advance, and it also provides any other necessary services to the senate, including any special meetings that might be necessary on short notices. The president or the vice president usually are facilitator and help in the smooth conduct of the meetings. The faculty senate may decide on policy issues with respect to appointment, promotion, and tenure, or it may recommend for the creation of new positions or eliminate old positions that may become obsolete, *but it does not decide on actual appointment, promotion, tenure, or termination.*

At each tier of the shared governance system, the meeting is divided into two sections: (1) unrestricted; and (2) restricted. Student representatives do not attend the restricted part—that is usually conducted after the completion of the unrestricted part. At the beginning of the restricted section meeting, the chair asks the student representatives to leave the meeting with a vote of thanks for their attendance. For each section, a separate minute of the meeting is produced—the unrestricted minutes in white papers and restricted minutes in pink or another color papers for easy identification and distribution to appropriate actors.

ACADEMIC FREEDOM

One issue of concern that I have heard from colleagues while working for a senate constitution committee and elsewhere is the question of academic freedom. Many faculty believe that working jointly with the administration can be intimidating because some faculty may not participate in the discussion or may be scared of opposing the administration's point of views when the meeting is presided over by the president or the vice president. This fear is baseless because there are many faculty colleagues as members of the committee against a single administrator—the vice president. So both these groups, while working for a common interest, take the most appropriate and equitable decisions. If we want a real shared governance process, no one should feel scared or shy to discuss relevant issues and points while decision is being made for the general good of the institution rather than in the interest of any individual or groups. Matters are being presented, described, and discussed, and a consensus decision is taken by the majority of the faculty. When consensus fails, a vote is taken, and no one can be taken into task for any opposing or supporting positions and views or descent. In fact, it is like the U.S. Congress that all decisions are made after debate, research, and discussion. In fact, in this all-inclusive shared management process the administration cannot take unilateral decision on hiring, firing, promotion, and tenure cases—the decision is taken jointly by the process discussed under 2c above. In this system, academic freedom is totally incorporated into the proposed shared governance system.

The other advantage of this system will be the reduction of court cases that often occurs in the USA because of some unilateral decisions. When decisions are made in a body, it is less likely that it would favor or disfavor anybody. For this reason, distribution of meeting papers are made well in advance so that each, and every member do their homeworks and come to the meeting well prepared to discuss matters of concern and interest. It is the management who assures the other party that no one gets into trouble while discussing problem issues or voting one or the other way. If freedom of expression cannot be protected in any decision-making process, then there is no need to have any shared governance in place.

CONCLUSION

I call the proposed shared governance processes as an ideal system if followed as suggested it encompasses all groups of actors in the decision-making process of an educational institution. All academic staff, the top management personal, and the student representatives are directly involved in academic and personnel decision for the faculty and academic decisions for the students. Under this system, top management cannot be blamed for any decision because all decisions are taken jointly. The faculty cannot also blame the administration for not being transparent. The practice of this system, as far as the personnel issues are concern, will have less chance of litigation as each case is scrutinized at three different levels—the department, the school, and the final authority, the trustee board or the board of visitors for any personnel decision. For any complicated personnel cases, before any decision is taken, legal guidance is sought, and then the decision is taken by the schools or the highest body. This process also eliminates one stage—the administration does not have to wait for the faculty senate's decision before it can take its decision because it has already been decided jointly. So this process is less time consuming. Another important area is the fact that under current system, the faculty senate ignores the administrators totally because none of the chain of administration is member of the senate. Administration has to wait until the senate or its committees decide cases before it (the administration) can consider and give its decision. That is why I call the current system to be based on the principles of employee union.

As is the case with any ideal process, the reality is dependent on actors. It is like Weber's principles of ideal bureaucracy that helps the social organizations to achieve their goals without favoring anyone. Against the principle of ideal bureaucracy at times, some actors bend some rules here and here to achieve or help common goals or actors as long as it does not favor the involved actors directly or indirectly. So will be the ideal shared governance system.

BIBLIOGRAPHY

Arenson, K. W. (1997). "From Dante's Inferno to Hot Seat at CUNY." The New York Times, June 9.

Arnold, G. (2000). The Politics of Faculty Unionization: The experience of Three New England Universities. Westport, Connecticut: Bergin and Garvey.

Association of Governing Boards of Universities & Colleges. (1996). "How to Create Lasting Change." Trusteeship 4:4 (26-29).

Benjamin, R. and S. J. Carroll. (1996). "Impediments and Imperatives in Restructuring Higher Education." Educational Administration Quarterly 32 (705-719).

Bing, R. and L. Dye. (1996). "Memo to the board of trustees: please meddle." Academe 82:4 (44-45).

Birnbaum, R. (1989). The Latent Organizational Functions of the Academic Senate: Why Senates Do Not Work But Will Not Go Away. In Peterson, M. (Ed.) "Organization and Governance in Higher Education" (1991, pp. 195-207). Needham Heights MA: Simon and Schuster.

Callan, P. M. 1995. "Trouble in UC's House of Lords." Los Angeles Times, July 19.

Clark, B. R. (1997). "Small Worlds, Different Worlds: The Uniqueness and Troubles of American Academic Professions." Daedalus 126:1 (21-42).

Cowley, W. H. (1980). Presidents, Professors, and Trustees: The Evolution of American Academic Government. San Francisco: Jossey-Bass.

Epstein, L. D. (1974). Governing the University. San Francisco: Jossey-Bass.

Finn, C. E. Jr. and B. V. Manno. (1996). "What's Wrong with the American University?" The Wilson Quarterly 20:1 (44-53).

Gergen, K. (1993). Organizational Theory in the Postmodern Era. In C. Brown (Ed.), Organization and Governance in Higher Education (2000), 5th ed., pp. 523-536). Boston: Pearson Custom Publishing.

Gilmour Jr., J. (1991). Participative Governance Bodies in Higher Education: Report of a National Study. New Directions for Higher Education 75, pp. 27-39.

Hardy, C. (1990). Putting Power into University Governance. In J. Smart (Ed.), Higher Education: Handbook of Theory and Research VI (pp. 393-426). New York: Agathon Press.

Healy, P. (1995). "Fiscal Firebrand." The Chronicle of Higher Education, November 10.

Healy, P. (1996a). "Minnesota Tackles the Possibilities and Problems of a Public College Merger." The Chronicle of Higher Education, December 20.

Healy, P. (1996b). "The Republican Contract with Public Colleges." The Chronicle of Higher Education, January 26.

Healy, P. (1996c). "A Shrewd Politician Assumes Presidency of University of Massachusetts." The Chronicle of Higher Education, April 19.

Healy, P. (1996d). "Single-Governing Board Is Proposed in Minnesota." The Chronicle of Higher Education, December 13.

Healy, P. (1996e). "Virginia's Council of Higher Education Becomes the Focus of a Power Struggle." The Chronicle of Higher Education, November 1.

Healy, P. (1996f). "Activist Republican Trustees Change the Way Public Universities Seek Presidents." The Chronicle of Higher Education, August 6.

Healy, P. (1997a). "Alabama Commission Proposes Major Cuts in Spending on Higher Education." The Chronicle of Higher Education, July 25.

Healy, P. (1997b). "Leaders of California's Two-Year College System Say Governance Structure Is at a Breaking Point." The Chronicle of Higher Education. December 19.

Healy, P. (1997c). "A Dismissal in Virginia." The Chronicle of Higher Education, May 16.

Healy, P. (1997d). "Report Calls for Strong State Coordination of Public Colleges." The Chronicle of Higher Education, June 27.

Healy, P. (1997e). "Showdown Pits Popular Governor against University of Kentucky." The Chronicle of Higher Education, May 30.

Healy, P. (1997f). "A Take-No-Prisoners Approach to Changing Public Higher Education in Massachusetts." The Chronicle of Higher Education, December 5.

Hines, E. R. and Hartmark, L. S. (1980). Politics of Higher Education. AAHE-ERIC Higher Education Research Report No. 7. Washington DC: American Association for Higher Education.

Hines, E. (2000). The Governance of Higher Education. In J. C. Smart & W. G. Tierney (Eds.), Higher Education: Handbook of Theory and Research, XV, (pp. 105-155). New York: Agathon Press.

Hines, E. R. and Hartmark, L. S. (1980). Politics of Higher Education. AAHE-ERIC Higher Education Research Report No. 7. Washington DC: American Association for Higher Education.

Hodgkinson, H. L. (1971). "Campus Governance: The Amazing Thing Is That It Works at All." Washington DC: ERIC Clearinghouse on Higher Education, Report No. 11.

Hodgkinson, H. L. (1974). "The Campus Senate: Experiment in Democracy." Berkeley: Center for Research and Development in Higher Education.

Hodgkinson, H. L. (1968). "Current Alternatives in Campus Governance." Berkeley: Center for Research and Development in Higher Education.

Hodgkinson, H. L. (1968). "Governance and Factions: Who Decides Who Decides?" Berkeley: Center for Research and Development in Higher Education.

Hodgkinson, H. L. and L. R. Meeth. (1971). Power and Authority: The Transformation of Campus Governance. San Francisco: Jossey-Bass.

Hollander E. (1994). "Coordinating Boards Are Under Attack." Trusteeship 2:4 (17-19).

Honan, W. H. (1994). "New Pressures on the University." The New York Times. January 4.

Horn, R. N. and R. T. Jerome. (1996). "When Corporate Restructuring Meets Higher Education." Academe 82:3 (34-36).

Ingram, R. T. (1993). Governing Public Colleges and Universities. Washington DC: AGB.

Ingram, R. T. (1996). "New Tensions in Academic Boardrooms." Trusteeship 4:6 (11-15).

Jones, G. A. and M. L. Skolnik. (1997). "Governing Boards in Canadian Universities." The Review of Higher Education 20:3 (277-295).

Jordan, M. (1993). "Universities Look to Streamlining, More Sharing of Resources." The Washington Post. November 21.

Kauffman, J. F. (1980). At the Pleasure of the Board: The Service of the College and University President. Washington DC: American Council on Education.

Keeton, M. 1977. "The Constituencies and Their Claims." In Governing Academic Organizations. G. L. Riley and J. V. Baldridge, Eds. Berkeley: McCutchan.

Keeton, M. (1971). Shared Authority on Campus. Washington DC: AAHE.

Keohane, N. O. (1996). "Boards Can't Pass the Buck." Trusteeship 4:2 (26-29).

Kerr, C. (1970). "Governance and Functions." Daedalus 99:1 (108-121).

Kerr, C. (19940). Higher Education Cannot Escape History: Issues for the Twenty-First Century. Albany: SUNY Press.

Kerr, C. (1994). Troubled Times for American Higher Education: The 1990s and Beyond. Albany: SUNY Press.

LaVista, D. J. and others. (1993). "A Senate Is a Senate Is a Senate?" Paper presented at the Annual Meeting, North Central Association, Chicago, April, 1993

Lazerson, M. (1997). "Who Owns Higher Education: The Changing Face of Governance." Change 29:2 (10-15).

Leatherman, C. (1994). "A Personnel Matter at Rutgers Flares into a Conflagration Over Governance." The Chronicle of Higher Education, December 14, A20.

Leatherman, C. (1998). "'Shared Governance' Under Siege: Is It Time to Revive It or Get Rid of It? The Chronicle of Higher Education, January 30, 1998, http.

Leatherman, C. (1998). "A New President for Adelphi." The Chronicle of Higher Education, March 13, A11.

Lee, B. 1980-81. Faculty Role in Academic Governance and the Managerial Exclusion: Impact of the Yeshiva University Decision. Journal of College and University Law, 7 (3-4), pp. 222-266.

Levin, J. (2000). What's the Impediment?: Structural and Legal Constraints to Shared Governance in the Community College. The Canadian Journal of Higher Education, XXX (2), pp. 87-122.

Leslie, D. W. (1996). "'Strategic Governance': The Wrong Questions?" The Review of Higher Education 20:1 (101-112).

Lewis, L. S. (1993). The Cold War and Academic Governance. Albany: SUNY Press.

MacTaggart, T. J. and Associates. (1996). Restructuring Higher Education: What Works and What Doesn't in Reorganizing Governing Systems. San Francisco: Jossey-Bass.

Magner, D. K. (1997). "University of Minnesota Faculty Rejects Union Despite Battle with Regents." The Chronicle of Higher Education, February 21.

McConnell, T. R. (1970). "Campus Governance and Faculty Participation." Berkeley: Center for Research and Development in Higher Education.

Miller, M. A. (1998). "Speed Up the Pace of Campus Governance or Lose the Authority to Make Decisions." The Chronicle of Higher Education, September 4, p. B6-7.

Miller, M. T. (1996). "The Faculty Forum: A Case Study in Shared Authority." Tuscaloosa: University of Alabama.

Miller, M. T. (1996). "Process and Task Orientations of Faculty Governance Leaders." Tuscaloosa: University of Alabama.

M. Miller and B. Kang. (1999). "International Dimensions to Shared Authority in Higher Education," 1999. *Review Journal of Philosophy and Social Science*, 24 (1/2), 69-82.

Miller, M. T., McCormack, T., and Newman, R. (1996). Faculty Involvement in Governance: A Comparison of Two Faculties. *The Journal of Staff, Program, and Organization Development*, 27.

G. Miller and M. Miller. (1997). "Shared Authority in Professional Education Governance: Roles and Desires of Full-Time Faculty," *Resources in Education, 32* (11), pp. 16

Miller, M. T., Newman, R. and Adams, T. (1999). Faculty Involvement in Academic Affairs. In M. T. Miller (Ed.), *Responsive Academic Decision Making: Involving Faculty in Higher Education Governance.* Stillwater, OK: New Forums Press.

Millett, J. D. (1984). Conflict in Higher Education: State Government Coordination versus Institutional Independence. San Francisco: Jossey-Bass.

Millett, J. D. (1980). *Management, Governance, and Leadership.* New York: American Management Association.

Millett, J. D. (1978). *New Structures of Campus Power.* San Francisco: Jossey-Bass.

Millette. Robert E. (2002). "Leadership and Shared Governance at Historically Black Colleges and Universities: Observations and Recommendations Provided an Overview of Academics and Governance at Black Colleges." Lincoln Journal of Social and Political Thought. Fall, Vol. 1. No. 1.

Newman, F. (1987). "Choosing Quality: Reducing Conflict between the State and the University." Denver: Education Commission of the States.

Newquist. D. C. (1998). "Does Moving with the Times Mean an End of Shared Governance?" The Chronicle of Higher Education, Letter to the Editor, March 13.

Novak. R. J. (1996). "Methods, Objectives, and Consequences of Restructuring." In Restructuring Higher Education. T. J. MacTaggart and Associates, Eds. San Francisco: Jossey-Bass,

Nussbaum, T. (1998). "Reforming the Governance of California Community Colleges." Twentieth Annual Earl V. Pullias Lecture in Higher Education. Mar. 14. (http://www.cccco.edu/cccco/gen/pullias.htm).

Perley, J. E. (1997). "Faculty and Governing Boards: Building Bridges." Academe 83:5 (34-37).

Pettit, L. K. and S. A. Kirkpatrick. (1984). "Combat Leaders without Troops." Educational Record 65:3 (4-7).

Ridgely, J. (1993). "Faculty Senates and the Fiscal Crisis." Academe 77:6 (7-11).

Riley, G. L. and J. V. Baldridge. (1977). Governing Academic Organizations. Berkeley: McCutchan.

Ruppert, S. S. (1994). Charting Higher Education Accountability. Denver: Education Commission of the States.

Scott, J. V. (1997). "Death by Inattention: The Strange Fate of Faculty Governance." Academe 83:6 (28-33).

St. John, E. P. (1995). "'Hard Decisions,' Retrenchment, and the Faculty Role." The NEA Higher Education Journal 21:1 (25-42).

Trani, E. P. (1997). "Creating a Broader Model of Shared Governance." The Chronicle of Higher Education, Point of View, January 10.

Wise, W. Max. (1970). "Reflections on New Configurations in Campus Governance." Paper presented at Annual Meeting, American Association for Higher Education, Chicago, March, 1970.

Wolfe, A. (1996). "The Feudal Culture of the Postmodern University." The Wilson Quarterly 20:1 54-66).

Wolvin, A. D. 1991. "When Governance Is Really Shared: The Multi-Constituency Senate." Academe 77:5 (26-28).

Strengthening Nigeria's Democracy through Investigative Reporting: Matters Arising

Olawuyi Ebenezer Adebisi
University of Ibadan, Nigeria

ABSTRACT

Among the critical component of an enduring democratic culture is a viable media whose systems and processes are derived from an unfettered engagement in reporting the society as the fourth estate of the realm. For the media to engage democracy as it should, it has to deeply understand the social, economic, and political dynamics that constantly interact to (re)define the democratic space. This understanding requires that the Nigerian media make an unwavering commitment in spite of *institutional* bottlenecks—real or imagined that plays itself to supplant or diminish the value of democratic governance. This, however, can be achieved when appropriate mechanisms for investigative culture are mainstreamed into the Nigerian media system. This notion is hinged on the premise that investigative reporting as a tool of responsible journalism can strengthen Nigeria's young democracy. Therefore, this paper examines the journalistic style and performances of Nigerian media vis-à-vis their role in strengthening the nation's nascent democracy with a view to making case for a newsroom policy framework that would consider as imperative investigative reporting as a bastion for sustainable participatory democracy.

INTRODUCTION

The evolution of democracy from the classical era to this contemporary time has grown to assume different persona. The adoption and subsequent domestication of this system of government has brought about variants of models, with each reflecting peculiar sociopolitical frameworks. Williams (2003), based on his conception and understanding of democracy, sees it either as an "idea" or as a "process." According to him, the notion of democracy being an "idea" is "deployed as an analytic concept, a normative ideal, a political prescription, and an empirical description." This position is derived from the thinking that democracy as a political concept is "essentially contested." Therefore, there cannot be a consensus on its core meaning. Because whatever meaning is adopted will depend on the way it is practiced and perceived in specific historical contexts. This perspective provides a point of convergence between historical narrative and conceptual analysis with which both historians and political philosophers tend to feel uncomfortable about. On the other hand, democracy as a process "explores the themes of nationalism, community, class, development, economic strategies, international debt, and multiparty elections and their implications for democratic politics." In a nutshell, democracy as an idea can be described as a notional concept, which derives its meaning from existing normative systems and processes; while as a process, it is the identification of components that make for the systemic running of the democratic institution without hitches.

In spite of disputations or contestations as it were on what constitutes a picture perfect democratic system, political philosophers and scientists are not at cross-purposes on the universal ethos of democracy, which significantly makes it the preferred system of government all over the world. This is underscored by the fact that in the people lies the power of self-determination of who rules/leads them. And this, to date, remains the underlying predicator for all political theorisation about the conceptual understanding of democracy.

Encyclopaedia Britannica describes democracy as a "form of government in which supreme power is vested in the people and exercised by them directly or indirectly through a system of representation usually involving periodic free elections." In a similar vein, Joseph Schumpeter's minimal description of democracy as "that institutional arrangement for arriving at political decisions in which individuals acquire the power to decide by means of a competitive struggle for the people's vote" (Williams, 2003) further drives home the point that the sovereignty of the people is actually the very bastion of democratic culture.

Therefore, to argue that no single conception of democracy can have priority over all others is not to imply that each conception is as good as any other. To the contrary, it is to bring out the need for "permanent dialogue" on the meaning of democracy, on the conditions for its existence, and on the criteria for defining and evaluating practices and institutions in specific historical contexts (Williams, 2003). This notwithstanding, it will not be out of place to assert that this form of government is perhaps the only "political system that allows for the dispersal of power and public access to it" (O'Neil, 1998). It clearly validates the age-long aphorism of democracy as espoused by Abraham Lincoln as a "government of the people, by the people, for the people."

While countries in the northern hemisphere may have taken the adoption of democratic culture as a way of life, emerging economies in the southern hemisphere, particularly African countries, are still grappling to come to terms with institutionalizing participatory democracy as a system of government. Even in countries where *democracy* is said to be practiced, the voice of the people is muffled and their will subverted through constitutional manipulations. If the Nigerian experience is taken as a case study, leadership in Africa comprises self-absorbed political elite with no properly conceived national project. They are totally engrossed in the quest for absolute and eternal power. They know only their interests. It is the only morality they have and their only religion. They hear only the echoes of their own voices and see only their images filling every space and consciousness (Ake, 1996). Little wonder the continent has earned the notoriety of being home to theaters of genocidal massacres; the most recent being the tragedy of Kenya, the country that prides itself as the beautiful land of the safari.

At any rate, all across sub-Saharan Africa, there is an evident and increasing support for the adoption of democratic political culture. This can be attributed to a response to both internal and external pressure, which drums support for the dismantling of political structures that excludes participation as well as representation of the citizens. For instance, the New Partnership for African Development (NEPAD), which became operational in 2001, "explicitly requires ascertainable progress toward more democratic and transparent systems." Similarly, the peer-review mechanism of the African Union (AU) is conceived as a platform "through which African countries are to reciprocally monitor each other's progress toward democracy" (Unegbu, 2003:42).

While these structures, to all intent, and purposes are commendable. It is unfortunate that the African Union, especially through its peer-review mechanism, is not likely to achieve much. This can be adduced to the fact that some of these leaders came to power through deeply flawed electoral systems and processes. It is only commonsensical that those who seek equity must do so with clean hands. How clean are the hands of our so called leaders? A case in point is Nigeria, where the late president and commander-in-chief of the Armed Forces, Alhaji Umar Musa Yar'Adua, openly admitted that the electoral process that brought him to power was not credible. Paradoxically, the election petition tribunal upheld his election. Although the judgement of the tribunal was appealed, the Supreme Court upheld the judgement of the election petition tribunal, which put paid to the controversies that surrounded the election. Nevertheless, this scenario only supports the fact that some African leaders lack the moral propriety to act as checks and balances or as peer-reviewers as the case may be on the pertinence of responsive and responsible governance in the continent. It is increasingly obvious that "elections in themselves may represent the fact of democratization, but they do not translate into democracy, the absence of which has brought continuing damage to the continent." Therefore, the "democratic project in Africa needs to be located within the province of the people's interest" avers Mr. Reuben Abati, former chairman, Editorial Board of *The Guardian* and the special adviser (Media and Publicity) to President Goodluck Ebelo Jonathan.

Nigeria's evolving and complex political landscape has provided scholars with numerous models and perspectives in the study of political organizations, social movement, and style of military governance. The attainment of political independence in October 1960 was presumed to be an initiation into the grand stand of participatory democracy as well as the push button that would fast track her developmental aspirations. This assumption was primarily predicated on such indicators as an emerging crop of Western-educated elites, increasing urbanization, vast resource endowment, and a prevailing consumer culture among the dominant class. In the light of this, Nigeria was hailed as the giant of Africa and the leading light that would provide social, economic, and political leadership in the continent. Unfortunately, however, post-independent realities suggest that "such expectations were a historical, shortsighted, and grossly unrealistic" (Ihonvbere and Vaughan, 1995).

Unegbu (2003) noted that since independence to date, Nigeria has implemented five constitutions under twelve leaders with majority of them having being midwifed by military dictators. He, however, pointed out that in spite of the stranglehold of the military on partisan politics, "there remains in Nigeria a deep and widespread commitment to democracy." Nigeria, therefore, is in a position to provide "the more credible litmus of democracy's future in sub-Sahara Africa . . . Thus, by strengthening its own fledgling democracy, Nigeria can take the first step to fortifying the same impulse elsewhere" (page 41).

NIGERIAN MEDIA, INVESTIGATIVE REPORTING AND DEMOCRACY

The essential role of the media in strengthening the pillars of democratic structure is not an issue that can be contested. However, more instructive is the functional role of the fourth estate of the realm in sustaining democracy. Viscount Rothermere, chairman of the *Daily Mail* and General Trust, noted that the survival of democracy is inextricably tied to freedom of speech and communication, and a free media was "democracy in action"; it is the natural way of managing change in society—and any repression of that right could lead to "explosion." In spite of these virtues, Lord Rothermere was quick to point out that the media have "all the human failings, thank God. It infuriates government; it angers special interests—but it angers them all equally." As a matter of fact, he concludes that "one thing is sure. You cannot have a democracy today without freedom of speech and of communication" (Noris, 2004).

The Nigerian media have a chequered history of engagement in political struggles. In fact, it can be said that the highpoint of the media's journalistic style and performance can be traced to their active involvement in fighting colonial government for the nation's independence. And in the post-independent Nigeria, the media, along with civil society organizations, have had to tackle military despots, redeeming the country from the military debacle. Former Governor Chimaroke Nnamani of Enugu State in a lecture titled "The Press and the Nigerian state" also placed in perspective the interventionist role of the Nigerian media thus:

> Nigerian press intervened at various stages of the nation's evolution. It also propped arguments for hope and continuity of the project, irrespective of such vitiating factors as *ethnicism, myopia, corruption, and ignorance.* In doing these, the press had set the stage, sometimes against the tide of national primo factors and so earned the wrath of friends of, or indeed, the powers that be.

Sankore (2007), appraising media resistance in Nigeria under the military, noted that "successive military regimes in Nigeria shared a common characteristic of repressing the media." He stated further that of all the sectors of the civil society that clamored for an end to military dictatorship, the media—after civil society organizations (CSOs)—paid the highest price. This is because the media reflected the voice of dissent in the absence of democratic structures such as parliament or opposition parties that could withstand the tyranny of the military adventurists. Because the media became the key arena for debate and the reflection of democratic voices, the military naively concluded that by censoring the media by any means possible, it could eliminate dissent, criticism, or opposition. The various regimes employed different tactics to no avail. "When carrots failed, batons, bullets, and dungeons were employed."

If the Nigerian experience is anything to go by, one may be quick to align with the position of Bennett (1998:195) that "free media systems are much better at bringing down authoritarian regimes than they are at later sustaining stable, participatory democracies." When the activities of the media are subjected to close scrutiny, especially between 1999 and now, they have not fared badly. But much still have to be done to ensure that the much touted *dividend of democracy* becomes tangible.

Assessing the functional role of the media between 1999 and 2007, Mr. Lanre Idowu, media critic and publisher of *Media Review,* noted that Nigeria's democracy is at its infancy. He said the 1999 constitution of the Federal Republic of Nigeria spells out that the art of governance is to seek the welfare of the people. Premised on this constitutional provision, he posits that for there to be good governance, "due process, rule of law, impartial judiciary, free and responsible press should be seen to be alive and active in the discharge of their responsibilities. Consequently, "for democracy to thrive, governance has to be monitored." It is instructive from the views expressed that there is a strong connection between media and enduring democratic culture. It is assumed that "for democracies to function, civil society requires access to information as a means to make informed political choices. Similarly, politicians require the media as a way in which they can take stock of the public mood, present their views, and interact with society. The media are thus viewed as a vital conduit of relations between state and society" (O'Neil, 1998).

In keeping with its fourth estate role, Waisbord (undated) makes case for the media to embrace investigative journalism. This brand of journalism "provides the first rough draft of legislation. It does so by drawing attention to failures within society's systems of regulation and to the ways in which those systems can be circumvented by the rich, the powerful, and the corrupt." Waisbord further explained that the media can take on this responsibility by holding:

> government accountable by publishing information about matters of public interest even if such information reveals abuses or crimes perpetrated by those in authority. From this perspective, investigative reporting is one of the most important contributions that the press makes to democracy. It is linked to the logic of checks and balances in democratic systems. It provides a valuable mechanism for monitoring the performance of democratic institutions as they are most broadly defined to include governmental bodies, civic organizations, and publicly held corporations.

Rusbridger (1999) attempts to place in perspective what *public interest* means within the contest of investigative reporting vis-à-vis good governance. According to him, "What's the public interest in a cricketer having a love romp in a hotel room or a rugby player having smoked cannabis twenty years ago? But if elected representatives are arguing a case in Parliament but not revealing that they are being paid to do so, then that strikes at the heart of democracy. That's public interest; this is an easy distinction." It is against this background that Katunmoya (2004:x) opines that if the media truly embrace their *watchdog* function fearlessly by going beyond routine, spot reporting to unravel "underhand dealings and clandestine schemes calculated to benefit the plotters to the disadvantage of the great majority . . ." such actions would undoubtedly stem the tide of abuse of office which have become familiar features of governance in this part of the world.

Perhaps the only time within Nigeria's current democratic experience that the media truly lived up to the billing by exposing a *fraudster* in government was in 1999 when *The News* investigated the certificate scandal of the then speaker of the House of Representatives, Alhaji Salisu Buhari, and found him guilty. After that major catch, nothing has happened. Even with allegations flying round, the media seem incapacitated to investigate. Why has it taken the media so long to come up with other catches? Is it that Nigeria has been rid of people of questionable characters walking the corridors of power?

There are so many questions begging for answers: unresolved assassinations (Pa Alfred Rewane, Chief Dikibo, Chief Bola Ige, former Attorney General and Minister of Justice, etc.); the missing fifty billion naira Police Equipment Fund (PEF); political corruption; the fraud that characterize April 2007 general elections, sixteen billion dollars unaccounted power project, etc. In all these, the media have not been able to come up with any substantial information, perhaps because their hands have been soiled in the process. It is high time the media realized the full import of their responsibility as the fourth estate of the realm. Therefore, for our democracy to work, the onus is on the media not to shy away from reporting "information about wrongdoing that affects the public interest."

In the absence of an articulate newsroom policy on investigative reporting that will protect political transitions, it is not surprising that fledgling "one person, one vote" democracies quickly become the prey of demagogues, nationalists, and authoritarians (Bennett, 1998: 204). In order to ensure that the democratic process is not hijacked by these self-professing democrats, Vreg's fourteen-point guidelines aimed at preventing freedom of the media from working against democratic development, and summarized by Bennett (1998) can be regarded as a roadmap for the media to selflessly pursue its social responsibility mandate. These are:

- Actively promote free and independent media as well as decentralization with guarantees for "communicative pluralism" (i.e., access for diverse groups) and "communicative federalism" (i.e., control of media by these groups);
- Design media policies to favor public participation in communication management;
- Limit the domination of the domestic media by global conglomerates while encouraging the flow of external ideas into the polity.

The implementation of the above proposals indicates the firming up of the capacity of the media to engage in the task of nation-building, particularly as it relates to good political governance which democracy, in principle, advocates. It is believed, though arguably, that these proposals also provide a conducive environment for investigative reporting to thrive.

THE HEART OF THE MATTER

The need to strengthen Nigeria's democratic fortunes has appropriately being emphasized. The fact of this submission is anchored on two critical assumptions, which can be classified under internal and external: internally, a genuine democratic system would offer the country "the best conditions for economic development," provide Nigerians with the chance to live under a regime of fair laws enacted in the national interest as opposed to the familiar tyranny of crude military despots," and lastly, "the evolution of a culture of debate and the unfettered exchange of ideas, a process that can be energized by Nigeria's traditionally vigorous and outspoken free press" (Unegbu, 2003:43). On the external plane, Unegbu (2003:41) is of the opinion that "[s]hould democracy succeed there [Nigeria], it will dramatically improve chances for democracy elsewhere in sub-Sahara Africa."

In all these, the role of the media, unquestionably, cannot be underestimated. Baker (1998), cited in Chaplin and Knoedler (2006), noted that embedded in the surveillance function of the media is the crucial role of being a "watchdog." In other words, "while the role of the press is not to challenge governmental information or encourage direct participation by the public, the press does have a duty to inform the public fully about the actions taken by governmental elites and experts. This knowledge protects against corruption and incompetence." Again, as pointed out earlier, the media can only rise up to this hallowed responsibility through investigative reporting. The desirability of this form of journalism notwithstanding, and its invaluable potential at preserving the integrity of the democratic culture from being desecrated, Nigerian media seem far from ready to take up this challenge despite their unwavering commitment to the establishment, restoration, and continued survival of democracy in the country. It is in line with this position that I have identified certain factors, which by far are in no way exhaustive, what in the topic of this paper is catch-phrased "Matters Arising."

To start with, the issue of ownership of media in Nigeria constitutes a drawback to the practice of investigative reporting. Media owners are either government or private. In the case of government media, journalists engage in self-censorship in order to protect and keep their jobs. While the so-called privately owned media organizations are either owned by politicians or their cronies, and they depend largely on government patronage through advertisements, advertorials, and some cases, their proprietors are also registered contractors with government. This "unwholesome" relationship inhibits the media from critically assessing government activities. O'Neil (1998:1) noted that institutional checks and balances within the state structure are imperative as necessary firewalls against abuse of office by politicians. The media, acting as the fourth estate, "are expected to critically assess state action and provide such information to the public. Ideally, then, the media not only provide a link between rulers and the ruled but also impart information that can constrain the centralization of power and the obfuscation of illicit or unethical state action." Unfortunately, Nigerian media "have moved away from their watchdog role, choosing to form close ties with political elites and thus limiting the degree of critical analysis within the news."

The drive for profit, which is at the heart of the capitalist economy, is another fang that makes mainstreaming investigative reporting into the journalistic culture of the Nigerian media difficult. The media system is linked ever more closely to the capitalist system, both in terms of ownership and reliance upon advertising. According to Mcchesney (1999), "[C]apitalism benefits from having a formally democratic system, but capitalism works best when elites make most fundamental decisions, and the bulk of the population is depoliticized. For a variety of reasons, the media have come to be expert at generating the type of fare that suits, and perpetuates, the status quo." He argues that "if we value democracy, it is imperative that we restructure the media system so that it reconnects with the mass of citizens who in fact comprise 'democracy.'" Therefore, the Nigerian media should be reformed in such a way that it will constitute a "part of a broader political movement to shift power from the few to the many." I think the Political Reforms committee set up by President Umar Musa Yar'Adua should also place in perspective the role of the media in ensuring credible and transparent election in the years to come.

Most Nigerian media organizations pay pittance as remunerations to their staff, and this makes the attraction to compromise on the very tenets of the ethical code of the profession very high. It is disheartening to note that a reporter in Nigeria earns between twenty thousand naira and fifty thousand naira monthly—a "take-home pay that cannot take him home" (apology to the Academic Staff Union of Universities (ASUU) as he must have spent almost all in commuting himself to and from his place of work. A story was told of a publisher who sent a correspondent to an African country to file in report from that part of the continent. The journalist innocently asked what his pay would be since he would have to relocate and possibly move his family along with him. The publisher reacted with fury, calling the journalist an ingrate who didn't appreciate the privilege of working outside the country. According to the publisher, many Nigerian journalists would literally jump at the offer, considering it a once-in-a-lifetime opportunity. The story is also told of this same publisher who considers the identity cards he issues to his staff as their meal ticket, and so when pay is not forthcoming, they are not expected to complain. After all, the journalists should be smart enough to eke out a living through the *wonder* of his identity card. As a result of this experience and others not mentioned, it is not surprising, therefore, that journalists insist on being "motivated" before they cover or report events. It is equally not strange to find journalists on the payroll of politicians or doubling as spin doctors for them.

Since investigative reporting is remarkably different from routine journalism, it logically follows that it requires a specialized tool kit. Against this background, it is important that an investigative reporting *Guide Book* which spells in carefully outlined details, the steps, strategies, systems, and processes for carrying investigative reporting. This is particularly important as such book would provide the blueprint for carrying out the essential task of journalism as vital ingredients for effective governance. Oso (2007), making case for guide book, said it is necessary to provide direction on the best ways to doing things, how to use journalism to assist the country's governance, and to help move the profession forward. Thus, putting in place a guide book is likely to provide the needed "guide" that would enable the journalist to operate within the ambits of the law and acceptable ethical traditions.

Based on the overarching and extreme importance of investigative reporting to good governance, it is imperative that journalists who would tow this path must exhibit certain character and personality traits which are remarkable ingredients for the successful pursuit of this brand of journalism. The conceptual framework of investigative reporting can only be achieved when certain structures are in place within the media organizations. It is the availability of such structures that would point to the readiness of the media to want to pursue investigative journalism with fearless conviction. Mr. Lanre Arogundade, coordinator, International Press Centre, Lagos, Nigeria, advocates for a newsroom policy that would primarily cater to the adoption of the investigative culture by the Nigerian media. This policy, among others, should make adequate provision for the:

- Establishment of Investigative desks in all media organizations whose primary responsibility will be to carry out investigation on pertinent issues;
- Provision/access to investigative resources such as time (to do painstaking work), money (for travels), high-tech communication gadgets, open records/access to information laws, research assistance, training in interview techniques, training in Computer Assisted Reporting (CARS); and
- Institution of reward systems that will reduce the temptation of journalists to compromise the integrity of the profession.

Mr. Arogundade is of the opinion that a newsroom policy framework is an excellent tool for building an enduring investigative culture. It is essentially an editorial code, which should emanate from in-house debates and agreements derived from analysis involving reporters, sub-editors, photographers, cartoonists, editorial board members, editors, managing editors, editors-in-chief. It explains what the journalist investigates, i.e., ongoing/unreported stories.

The official Secret Acts is an initiative by the government of Nigeria to restrict access to information or document at the disposal of government. With this act, the journalist is incapacitated to access any information/ document that could facilitate his investigation. It is against this background that the Freedom of Information (FOI) bill was sponsored by a coalition of civil society organizations to make government accountable to the people. Unfortunately, since 1999, that bill was presented to the House of Assembly; to date, no tangible action has been taken on it. It is apparent from all indications that the *powers that be* fear the passage of the bill into law. As a matter of fact, the Freedom of Information empowers the media to access information about the workings of the government. For investigative journalism to therefore thrive, concerted pressure should be mounted on the National Assembly to expedite action on the passage of the bill without further delay.

Another issue that urgently begs for attention as parts of the framework for strengthening our fledgling democracy through investigative reporting is rethinking the curriculum of journalism institutions in Nigeria. It is important that institutions such as monotechnics, polytechnics, and universities offering journalism courses should accord the teaching of investigative journalism priority in the scheme of things. Pate (2007) noted that the bane of journalism training in Nigeria is that the curriculum is based on western conceptual and theoretical underpinnings. Potential journalists are therefore trained using foreign models which they find absolutely difficult to contextualize within our social reality. He, however, suggested that in strengthening our training capacities, there is the need to fully expose our students to the history, systems, dynamics, geography, successes, and challenges of the Nigerian nation. Besides, they need to be equipped with the right skills as well as sensitized to appreciate their unique roles as professional journalists within the context of a developing country in a globalizing world.

The individual journalist also has a role to play in upholding the "right of the public to know." Frost (2000:1) says the "journalist's tussles are going to be between the right of the public to know and some other moral tenet . . . which would militate against publication." This right of the public to know is predicated on the theory of democratic governance as espoused by John Stuart Mill. The implication is that each journalist has to decidedly demonstrate impregnable character traits that empowers "every citizen not only having a voice in the exercise of that ultimate sovereignty, but being, at least occasionally, called on to take an actual part in government, by personal discharge of some public function, local or general" (Mill, cited in Frost, 2000:1). The journalist can only do this when his personal interest is subordinated to the interest and well-being of the "entire aggregate of the community."

CONCLUSION

The issues raised above seem a tall order for the media given our peculiar normative clime. But when the benefits inherent in why our democracy needs investigative journalism to thrive are duly considered, which include: nurturing an informed citizenry who will ultimately hold the government accountable through voting and participation; important agenda-setting powers to remind citizens and political elites about the existence of certain issues; news about political and economic wrongdoing can trigger investigations by relevant bodies such as Code of Conduct Bureau, Economic and Financial Crimes Commission (EFCC), security agencies (Waisbord, undated), then, no sacrifice will be too much. As a matter of fact, the media can make the people have unblemished faith in the democratic institution by not only acting as the *watchdog* but also the *guard dog* of our nascent democracy. Unless the media are ready to mobilize the people to engage in large numbers with diverse processes of self-governance, democracy might end up as an empty shell that is devoid of substance and merely providing a veritable platform for self-seeking opportunists and political tyrants to hold sway (Krishna, 2002).

About two decades ago, "democracy and democratisation were promoted as the panacea for the failure of the African states." Today, it is obvious that to African leaders, "an election needs not be an expression of the people's will but only a mechanism for a contrived self-perpetuation in office" (Abati, 2008: 54). This anathema notwithstanding, democracy is not merely desirable; it is necessary. Understandably, it is not the solution to all our problems, but none of the major problem can be solved without it (Ake, 1996). Again, it is worth reiterating for the umpteenth time that "Nigeria provides the more credible litmus of democracy's future in sub-Saharan Africa." The Nigerian media sure have a role to play in the emergence of a new democratic Nigeria where transparency, accountability, and good governance are nonnegotiable.

REFERENCES

Abati, R. (2008) "Kenya Is Burning: Its Leaders Are Fiddling" in *The Guardian* Sunday, January 6, 2008, pp 54.

Ake, C. (1996) *Is Africa Democratizing?* (CASS Monograph No. 5). Lagos: Malthouse Press Limited

Arogundade, L. (2007) "Mechanism for Building an Investigative Culture in the Nigerian Media: The Case for Newsroom policy

Framework." Being text of a paper presented at a one-day mini conference on "News, Accountability, and Strengthening Nigeria's Democracy" organized by the Wole Soyinka Investigative Reporting Award (WSIRA) with support from Canadian International Development Agency (CIDA), Ostra Hotel, Ikeja, Lagos, December 28, 2007.

Champlin, D. P. and Knoedler, J. T (2006) "The Media, the News, and Democracy: Revisiting the Dewey-Lippman Debate." Journal of Economic Issues. Volume: 40. Issue: 1. pp 135+. Retrieved from www. questia.com on February 14, 2008.

De Burgh, H. (2000) "Investigative Journalism: Context and Practice." London: Routledge.

Foerstel, H. N. (1999) "Freedom of Information and the Right to Know: The Origins and Applications of the Freedom of Information Act." Westport, CT: Greenwood Press. Retrieved from www.questia.com on February 14, 2008.

Frost, C. (2000) *Media Ethics and Self-Regulation*. Harlow, England: Longman.

Idowu, L. (2007) "Engaging Democracy through an Investigative Reporting: An Assessment of the Nigeria Media Since 1999." Being text of a paper presented at a One-day mini conference on "News, Accountability, and Strengthening Nigeria's Democracy" organized by the Wole Soyinka Investigative Reporting Award (WSIRA) with support from Canadian International Development Agency (CIDA), Ostra Hotel, Ikeja, Lagos, December 28, 2007.

Ihonvbere, J. and Vaughan, O. (1995) "Nigeria: Democracy and Civil Society: The Nigerian Transition Programme, 1985-1993." In John A. Wiseman (ed.) Democracy and Political Change in Sub-Saharan Africa. New York: Routlege. Retrieved from www.questia.com on February 14, 2008.

Kantumoya, L. M. (2004) *Investigative Reporting in Zambia: A Practitioner's Handbook.* Lusaka: Transparency International Zambia and Friedrich Ebert Stiftung.

Krishna, A. (2002) "Enhancing Political Participation in Democracies: What is the Role of Social Capital" in *Comparative Political Studies,* Vol. 35 No. 4. 2002, pp 437-460.

Mcchesney, R. W. (1999) "Are the Media Killing Democracy?" Free Inquiry. Vol. 20, Issue: 1. Retrieved from www.questia.com on February 14, 2008.

Nnamani, C. (2003) "The Press and the Nigerian Project." Being the text of a public lecture of the Newspaper Proprietors Association of Nigeria (NPAN) at Diamond Hall, Golden Gate Restaurant, Ikoyi, Lagos, on Thursday, October 23, 2003.

Norris, D. (1996) "The Vital Role a Free Media Plays in Any Democracy." *The Daily Mail.* February 15, 1996. Page Number: 26. Retrieved from www.questia.com on February 14, 2008.

O'Neil, P. O. (1998) "Communicating Democracy: The Media and Political Transitions." Boulder, CO: Lynne Rienner. Retrieved from www.questia.com on February 14, 2008.

Oso, L. (2007) "Structuring a Model Guidebook as Resource Support for Investigative Journalism in Nigeria: The Critical Factors to Consider." Being text of a paper presented at a one-day mini conference on "News, Accountability, and Strengthening Nigeria's Democracy" organized by the Wole Soyinka Investigative Reporting Award (WSIRA) with support from Canadian International Development Agency (CIDA), Ostra Hotel, Ikeja, Lagos, December 28, 2007.

Pate, U. A. (2007) "Strengthening Media Capacity for Investigative Journalism through Institutions' Based Curriculum." Being text of a paper presented at a one-day mini conference on "News, Accountability, and Strengthening Nigeria's Democracy" organized by the Wole Soyinka Investigative Reporting Award (WSIRA) with support from Canadian

International Development Agency (CIDA), Ostra Hotel, Ikeja, Lagos, December 28, 2007.

Sankore, R. (2007) "Media Resistance in Nigeria: *The News* and *Tempo*" in *50 Years of Journalism: African Media since Ghana's Independence.* California: The African Editors' Forum, Highway Africa and Media Foundation for West Africa in Johannesburg, South Africa. pp. 26-30.

Unegbu, C. O. (2003) "Nigeria: Bellwether of African Democracy" in *World Policy Journal.* Volume XX, No. 1, Spring 2003. pp. 41-47.

Waisbord, S. (undated) "Why Democracy Needs Investigative Journalism" in *Media Ethics.* Compiled by Whitney M. Young Jr. Information Resource Center Public Affairs Section, U.S. Consulate Lagos, Nigeria.

Williams. G. (2003) "Democracy as Idea and Democracy as Process in Africa." The Journal of African American History. Volume: 88. Issue: 4. Retrieved from www.questia.com on February 14, 2008.

Questioning the Traditional Model for Training Clinical and Counseling Psychologists: Why Treatment Efficacy Rates Are Low and Psychological Evaluations Inaccurate

David B. Stein, Ph.D.
Virginia State University

INTRODUCTION

This article explores several issues surrounding the American Psychological Association's standards for accrediting doctoral training of clinical/counseling psychologists. Three issues will be addressed in this paper. First, the issue of treatment efficacy rates will be explored. Second, the validity and reliability data on several of the more frequently used psychology tests will be reviewed. Third, the actual course content of 115 American Psychological Association approved doctoral programs will be reviewed. There are three hypotheses to be addressed:

1. Psychosocial treatment efficacy rates are low for most human problems. There may be a few bright sparks, but they appear to be the exception.
2. Validity and reliability of psychological tests are low, almost worthless, and are therefore, considered dangerous and misleading. It is also hypothesized that current reviews indicate that tests previously favored and considered fairly valid are more recently viewed by updated research as invalid and unreliable, most notably the Minnesota Multiphasic Personality Inventory (MMPI). Additionally, it is hypothesized that examination of current course content indicates that the vast majority of graduate

schools are still teaching assessment courses predicated on a foundation of invalid and unreliable test materials.

3. Doctoral training has changed little since its inception in the early 1900s, clinging to a model that is mostly theoretical, abstract, and arcane, with little emphasis on treatment strategies for specific human problems.

CONTROVERSY OVER TREATMENT EFFICACY RATES

Eysenck (1952, 1961) upset the psychological world when he pioneered research on psychological treatment efficacies. His research indicated that individuals with a host of behavioral and emotional problems improved better over time when they did not visit a therapist, while those who sought psychological help did worse. Numerous studies followed, with most supporting his findings. A large scale meta-analysis by Lipsey and Wilson (1993) does not seem to clear the confusion over efficacy rates. On the one hand, the authors make the following statement:

> It is a distressing observation that, over recent decades, the results of treatment research and reviews of that research have not yielded convincing support for the efficacy of many psychological, educational, and behavioral treatments. (p. 2)

However, they later conclude that there are some positive effects with some of the treatments, namely cognitive/behavioral but only with those research projects conducted under careful research or quasi-research frameworks. Thus, "real world" or field studies are less efficacious, which is similar to Eysenck's conclusions.

Rossi and Wright (1984) concluded that:

> Similar controversy has characterized intervention in social work, counseling, education, criminal justice, organizational development, and a host of related areas echoed many reviewers in these areas when described evaluation research as a "parade of close-to-zero effects." (p. 348)

The Lipsey and Wilson (1993) meta-analysis seems to indicate that cognitive/behavioral treatments faired best. However, for purposes of this study Stein observed the actual practices of twelve therapists who claimed to practice cognitive/behavioral treatments, where he found that all of them were, indeed, not faithfully practicing the methods espoused in the text and research literature, such as Beck (1961, 1979), Ellis and Harper (1975), Meichenbaum (1977), Maultsby (1984), and Kendall and Hollon (1981). In fact, it appeared that most were practicing a more home spun, common sense, and *made-up at the moment* variety. Eclectic would be insufficient to describe the observations.

Table 1

Some Treatment Efficacy Rates:
How effective are psychological/psychiatric treatments?

Problem	Efficacy
sex offenders	.05 (Hagen, 1997; Dineen, 2000)
physical abusers	.37 (Hagen, 1997)
criminals, general	.20 (Barlow & Durrand, 2006)
alcohol and drug abuse	.20 (Peele, 1995) including AA
marriage counseling	.33 (McGraw, 2000; Wilson, 2002)
counseling, general	.30 (Eysenck, 1952; Dineen, 2000)
oppositional teens	.20 (Stein, 2004)
conduct disorders	.17 (Stein, 2004)

Table 1 gives a brief idea of treatment efficacy rates for some of the more common forms of human problems. More extensive reports can be found in the Lipsey and Wilson (1993) meta-analysis where some efficacy rates are reported as being higher, i.e., cognitive/behavioral in pure academic form at .61, while others are reported as being even lower. Overall, treatment efficacy in the *field or real world* appears to be discouraging. Hagen (1997) reports that, when making threat assessments, psychologists are wrong two out of three times. Something is very wrong, and it is believed that a considerable part of the problem is in the actual course content of doctoral graduate training, which will be reviewed shortly.

BEHAVIOR MODIFICATION:
A RESPONSE TO THE EYSENCK STUDIES

It is interesting to note that following the Eysenck studies in the 1960s, it was suspected that the problem lay in nonempirically based treatments (Barlow and Durrand, 2006). Therefore, attention turned to the one treatment modality that spawned from learning theory research and later evolved into research-based treatments known as Behavior Modification and Behavioral Therapy (Kanfer and Phillips, 1970). Later, as a result of Meichenbaum's (1977) recognition of Ellis's Rational/Cognitive approaches, behavioral devotees adopted the cognitive concepts, and Cognitive/Behavioral Therapy resulted.

At first, it appeared as if psychological therapies were finally on an empirically based track. However, enthusiasm seemed to wane after some initial promising approaches appeared, such as with children (Patterson, 1971); Becker, Engelmann, and Thomas (1971), with desensitization for phobias (Wolpe, 1958) or Bandura's (1969) modeling approaches. It seemed that this enthusiasm was shortlived. A few treatment approaches have remained as standard, but for the most part, treatment efficacy rates with children and teenagers actually declined (Stein, 2001a), while other methods, such as covert sensitization (Barlow, Leitenberg, and Steinbrook, 1969) did not prove as promising as originally thought. When asked what went wrong with the behavioral movement, Eisler simply responded that "they ran out of ideas" (in a personal communication, September 28, 1997). Thus, the behavioral movement is still around, but it has not proven as the panacea to save the treatment efficacies of psychology. However, there is still hope that more and more research in the cognitive/behavioral arena for *specific human problems* will still prove to be more promising and even more importantly the work that now exists may be more incorporated into the training and reading requirements within doctoral programs.

THE VALIDITY OF PSYCHOLOGICAL TESTS

Psychology tests or what constitutes a *so-called battery of psychological tests* can be divided into three parts (Lilienfeld, S. O., Lynn, S. J., and Lohr, J. M., 2003):

1. One part is composed of *educational tests* that purportedly measure specific learning skills, such as reading, math, and writing, and the overall measure of *intelligence*, which is usually reported in the form of IQ, intelligence quotient score(s).
2. Second are the so-called personality tests, which in turn are divided in subjective personality tests and objective personality tests.
3. Third are the questionnaire-rated scales used to measure a plethora of things, such as attention deficit disorder, ADD; attention deficit hyperactivity disorder, ADHD; oppositional defiant disorder, ODD; conduct disorders; depression; and anxiety; all of which only scratches the surface at the countless number of questionnaires being produced at factory line rates.

EDUCATIONAL TESTS

Educational tests can measure weaknesses in a child's academic skills, but unfortunately, these weaknesses are increasingly being viewed as psychiatric diseases. Please note that the term disorder is often used, but modern lexicon has made this term, for most intents and purposes, synonymous to both the public and professional communities, with the term disease (Stein, 2001a, 2001b). Modern vernacular calls them *learning disabilities*, which reflects more accurately what they are (Strauss and Lehtinen, 1947). The same, which is to enlist a tutor to use what are called *multi-sensory learning methods* in order to properly relearn the fundamentals (Becker, W. C., Engelmann, S., and Thomas, D. R., 1971). It is the failure of not properly paying attention when the fundamentals are taught according to the World Health Organization.

Intelligence tests can also serve a useful purpose if they are properly used, but here, too, psychology bends the truth. The first intelligence test was developed by Alfred Binet and Theodore Simon in 1904 in France in order to estimate how well a child *might* do in an academic setting and therefore assist with the best class placement of a child. However, the IQ or intelligence quotient has over the years taken on a life of its own where it has come to mean that it becomes a true and accurate assessment of how intelligent a child actually is (Barlow and Durand, 2006); and once made, this label often sticks to the child for the rest of his life.

The reader is asked to consider how well an average farmer might do on such a test. Not well, one might guess, and yet the running of a farm requires nothing short of brilliance since it is such a complex endeavour; but once given, such labels tend to stick. Stein (2001a, 2001b, 2005) suggests that the term intelligence quotient, i.e., IQ, be replaced simply by RQ, i.e., readiness quotient, which is more apt and has considerable less stigma attached to it. Barlow and Durand (2006) state:

> One of the biggest mistakes nonpsychologists [and a distressing number of psychologists] make is to confuse IQ with intelligence . . . An IQ score significantly higher than average means that the person has a significantly greater than average chance of doing well in our educational system." (p. 75)

In sum, educational tests do measure specific skills and can be useful for identifying academic weaknesses.

PERSONALITY TESTS

We now enter the *Twilight Zone* of psychology. Hundreds of theories of personality exist, but no one has yet successfully identified or even defined what personality is (Hall and Lindzey, 1957). Thus, there exists a myriad of psychological tests that measure something that no one seems to quite know what it is. The first test that was introduced was the Rorschach Inkblot test, a *Projective Personality Test* introduced in 1921 by Swiss psychiatrist Hermann Rorschach, which consists of ten inkblots that were supposedly *carefully designed* in order to serve as psychology's equivalent to the x-ray (Wood, Nezworski, Lilienfeld, and Garb, 2003).

This of course begs the question of x-ray to what, something of which no one seems to know. It has no validity, with measures ranging between .03 and .28, which means that it does not predict behavior (Mischel, 1996; Wood et al., 2003), and it does not match with how individuals give self-reports. It also has no reliability (Mischel, 1996; Lilienfeld, Wood, and Garb, 2001a; Woods et al, 2003), which means that when individuals retake the test, they do not yield the same personality profiles.

The TAT, or Thematic Apperception Test, is the second most widely used projective test. It was developed in 1935 by Morgan and Murray at the Harvard Psychological Clinic. This test consists of a series of ambiguous drawings for which the test subject makes up a story and reports his feelings earlier, presently, and in the future that are related to the story. The examiner subjectively looks for themes and then reports his conclusions. The interpretation of this test is far less uniform than the Rorschach and turns out to be even less valid and less reliable (Lilienfeld, Wood, and Garb, 2000).

One hundred percent of the 115 graduate programs researched for this paper still teach courses in Rorschach and other projective testing techniques. Why? They are used 80 percent of the time by school psychologists (Lilienfeld, Wood, and Garb, 2000), and one third of the time in clinical practices and approximately over 80 percent for custody hearings, abuse and neglect hearing, and criminal trials (Lorandos and Campbell, 2005). Why? Presently, psychology is seeking to readopt the medical model probably in order to gain prescription writing privileges.

A different approach to personality testing was made with the introduction of *objective personality inventories.* This category of testing supposedly had a more empirical foundation. They were composed of specific questions which were made objective by administering and standardizing them against clinically based normative groups. An individual's answers were then compared to the normative group responses, yielding a supposedly *objective* profile. The most notable of these tests is the MMPI, or the Minnesota Multiphasic Personality Inventory, introduced by Hathaway and McKinley in 1943. Initially, the MMPI offered considerable promise as psychology's *x-ray* into the personality of subjects. However, one of the most prolific writers on psychological tests, Anne Anastasi (1988), began to question the validity of the test. She states, "The test manual and related publications now caution against literal interpretation of the clinical scales" (p. 530). Lilienfeld, Lynn, and Lohr (2003) report validity coefficients ranging from .29 to .37, which, to those familiar with correlation coefficients, really means that they are meaningless (Hagen, 1997). Anastasi (1988) stated, "The MMPI is essentially a clinical instrument whose proper interpretation calls for considerable psychological sophistication" (p. 531). However, this is not consistent with Lilienfeld, Lynn, and Lohr's (2003) more recent statement, "That is, clinicians with more MMPI experience and knowledge were no more accurate in their interpretations of MMPI data than were clinicians with significantly less MMPI experience and knowledge." Again, Lilienfeld, Lynn, and Lohr's (2003) point out that "similarly, experienced clinicians are generally no more accurate than advanced graduate students" (p. 24).

Other less popular tests have fared even worse (Anastasi, 1988). All this begs the questions as to why psychologists are wasting so much valuable training time on arcane, unproductive, invalid, unreliable, and inaccurate courses. Cannot their time be better spent reading intensely on the literature that is available on specific human problems where the student becomes intimately familiar with the all aspects of the problem, such as precipitants, effects on the family constellation and interactions, effects on the individual, the resulting cognitive and behavioral impairments, and treatment methods that empirically appear to be the most productive? What is taking so long for tenacious adherence to tradition to die out? Medicine has evolved since 1900; why has not psychology?

RATING SCALES AND QUESTIONNAIRES

Rating scales and questionnaires are being mass produced at factory production line rates (Stein, 2004). Rating scales and questionnaires are merely uniform interviews; they are not tests that yield insights into the human psyche, brain, mind, or soul. Most of them are used merely to approximate diagnoses from the *DSM-IV.* The problem is further complicated by the fact that there is little reliability between clinicians for making specific diagnoses (Davison and Neale, 1994; Lorandos and

Cambell, 2005). The inter-rater reliability statistics in the *DSM-III* were so low and embarrassing that the compilers of the *DSM-IV* handle the problem by merely eliminating all of the inter-rater statistics, and without reliability, there can be no validity (Lorandos and Campbell, 2005).

Unfortunately, questionnaires and rating scales are snuck into the so-called battery of psychological tests resulting in pronouncements to patients or parent of child or adolescent patients that they *have such and such a disorder*. If there are no medical tests and no psychological tests to make or confirm almost all psychiatric diagnoses, then how can questionnaires and rating scales approximate accurately that which does not exist?

FITTING THE DIAGNOSIS TO JUSTIFY PRESCRIPTIONS OF PSYCHIATRIC DRUGS

A new trend is emerging where diagnoses are being made to justify or change the use of psychiatric drugs. If a child is not responding to the stimulant drugs for ADD/ADHD, then parents may be told that their child is Bipolar (Papolos and Papolos, 2002) in order to justify switching drugs to the mood stabilizers (Stein, 2005). Adults who may be exhausted from long work hours and unending personal stresses may be told that they are depressed, which means that they have a chemical imbalance that can be remedied with antidepressants (Valenstein, 1998). The fact is that these drugs do not remedy any chemical imbalance (Breggin, 2002; Valenstein, 1998); they merely simultaneously stimulate and sedate, which helps the patient cope with life's stresses. The unfortunate problem is that if taken for long periods of time, these drugs can be extremely hazardous to health (Mosby, 2006).

HUMAN PROBLEMS

Before reviewing the course content of all APA accredited schools, it may prove useful to list some of the numerous problems with which the human race must cope:

Table 2

Types of Human Problems

Marriage	Religion (s)	Spousal abuse	Substance abuse and addictions
Divorce	Death and dying	Child abuse	Process addictions, i.e., addiction to behaviors, such as gambling, sex, pornography, and
Grief	Terrorism	Anger and temper tantrums	Excessive partying
Parenting	Homeland security	Sexual dysfunction(s)	Cultural, ethnic, and minority issues
Daily hassles or stresses	Crime and criminology	Depression and sadness	Prejudice, racial, and ethnic hatreds
Work-related stresses	The elderly	Existential and philosophical problems, such as finding a meaning and purpose for life	Conflict resolution
Communication and effective listening skills	Coping with having a handicapped child	Irrational and cognitive dysfunction	Effective behavior modification and therapies for specific problems, such as autism,
Assertiveness	Delinquency	Obesity and other eating disorders	Retardation and phobias
Psychopharmacology, with an emphasis on deleterious complications and side effects	Overcoming growing up with a highly dysfunctional family	Crisis intervention	Sociological problems of urban and rural living
Gangs	Cults	Prostitution	Gender issues for men and women
Overcoming shyness			

(This list is generated in part from Santrock, Minnett, and Campbell, 1994)

The list can go on and on. Readings for almost any of these problems are plentiful and inexhaustible. In addition, there are countless research and scientifically based studies in cognitive and behavioral psychology that already exist for each of these problem areas, but clinicians either do not know the material, are not trained in the material, or are ignoring the material in what they practice (Begley, 2009). *Courses involving extensive reading and extensive practice and rehearsal for dealing with as many of these problems as possible should consume the limited years that doctoral students have. Alas, such is not the case!*

COURSE CONTENT OF 115 APA ACCREDITED DOCTORAL PROGRAMS

This section is devoted to an extensive and comprehensive review of the course content of 115 APA, American Psychological Association, accredited doctoral programs. Data for five programs was not available. Hopefully, inaccuracies were avoided; but because this is such a formidable project, it is certain that some error has occurred. However, the overall course patterns are apparent, and it is judged that a few oversights would not alter the interpretation and analysis for the reader. The reader is asked to review the tables with care.

The first column lists the type of courses, and the right column lists the number of doctoral programs offering the courses. Please note that Assessment and Psychometrics upon close examination appear to mean the same thing, i.e., the administration of psychological tests.

Table 3

Total Core Course Offerings by all APA Accredited Doctoral Programs

N = 115

University Courses Offered	Total
Assessment	98
Psychopathology	94

Psychological Intervention	86
Psychometrics	59
Research Design	78
Research Methods	79
Statistics	78
Learning	47
Physiological Psychology	59
History and Systems	54
Social Psychology	63
Developmental Psych	58
Ethics	75
Practicum	81
Dissertation	71
Health Psychology	16
Personality Theories	50
Neuropsych	49
Neuropharmacology	18
Cognition	57
Advanced Human Memory	6

Child Psychology	6
Perception	32
Doctoral Project	3
Theory and Philosophy	30
Psychology as a Profession	13
Psychopharmacology	19
Personal Counseling	1
Motivation	12
Psycholinguistics	13
Group and Organizational Dynamics	8
Ego Psych	2

Object Relations	1
Animal Behavior	5
Community Psych	7
Psychophysics of Hearing	3
Drugs and Behavior	1
Visual Processes	5
Decision-Making Process	6
Comparative Psych	3
Experimental Psych	3
School Psych	5
General Psych	1
Helping Skills	1
Needs Assessment Techniques	1

Table 4

Total Elective Course Offerings By All APA Accredited Doctoral Programs

N = 115

University Courses Offered	Total
Cognitive Psychology	18
Perception	12
Motivation and Emotion	10
Developmental Psychology	19
Learning Processes	13
Social Psychology	18
Group Dynamics	7
Cardiology Seminar	1
Personality Theories	11

Neuropsychology	18
Theory and Research in Emotion	2
Dynamics of Pain	1
Seminar in Language Development	2
Health Psychology	9
Human Brain Behavior Relationships	1
Neurophysiology	16
Animal Behavior	3
Invertebrate Psychology	1
Design of the Mind	2
Drugs, Brain, and Behavior	6
Animal Human Communication	3
Language Acquisitions	7
Psycholinguistics	4
Moral Development	3
Social Influence	2
Behavioral Medicine	7
Social Oppression	1
Human Judgment	1
Hormones and Behavior	1
Cooperation and Competition	1
Contemporary Psychoanalytic Thought	1
History and Systems	4
Psychopharmacology	6
Mental Imagery	3
Independent Study	3
Media Psychology	1
Ego Psychology	1
Object Relations	1
Psych of a Typical Child	2
Objective Assessment	2
Environmental Psychology	2

Educational Psychology	2
Psych of Persuasion	1
Projective Assessment	2
Developmental Issues in Adolescent Girls	1
Suicide	1
Acculturation	1
Theological Concepts of Evil	1
Consumer Psychology	1
Readings in Psychology	7
Conflict Resolution	1

Table 5

Total Specialty Course Offerings By All APA Accredited Doctoral Programs

N = 115

University Courses Offered	Total
Teaching of Psychology	16
Rehabilitation Psychology/Vocational Rehab	2
Psychology of Aging	17
Motor Control After Stroke/Neurological Issues	2
Psychology of Addiction	14
Interviewing and Behavioral Observation	23
Behavioral Assessment	20
Interpersonal Psychotherapy	18
Behavior Therapy	32
Family/Marital Therapy	44
Child and Adolescent Psychotherapy	43
Forensic Psychology	8
Anxiety and Anxiety-Based Disorders	3
Organizational/Staffing/Personnel	23

Developmental Disabilities	8
Ethnic and Minority Issues in Psych/Diversity	49
Psychology of Sex Differences and Similarities/Gender	23
Sleep and Sleep Disorders	3
Youth and Violence	3
Psychology of Death and Loss	4
Issues in Rural Health	3
Stress, Coping, and Health	12
Law, Psychology, and Policy	9
Current Issues/Topics in Psychology	26
Supervision and Management	9
Psychology in the Community	26
Case Conference	3
Consultation Methods	8
Group Psychotherapy	32
Developing Scales/Instruments	3
Human/Computer Interaction	6
Expectations and Prevention of School Failure	1
Publication Seminar	1
Health Assessment and Major Illnesses	6
Health Education and Promotion	3
Crisis Intervention	3
Emotions and Health in Clinical Practice	2
Nonverbal Behavior	1
Intro to Rorschach	2
Hypnotherapy	2
Brief Psychotherapy	4
Bio Medical Data Programs	1
Play Therapy	1
Identification of Child Abuse	2
Psych and Deafness	1
Psych of Career Development	3
Minnesota Multiphasic Personality Inventory	1

Behavior Disorders of Childhood and Adol	1
Attitude and Attitude Change	12
Depression	4

The next three tables, Tables 3, 4, and 5, are summations of the overall course content of the 115 programs. Table 1 focuses on a summation of the core courses, which are usually taken during the first one or two years of doctoral work. Table 3 focuses on a summation of elective courses, which means that there is no assurance about which courses any individual doctoral student may have taken. Table 4 focuses on a summation of specialty course offerings, and again, what any individual student may have taken cannot be ascertained.

Immediately, it is apparent that extensive training in most of the human problems previously listed are absent in most programs. Psychological interventions may cover some of the topics, but interviews with numerous colleagues seems to indicate that these courses were mostly surveys of the more philosophical forms of therapies, such as Freudian, Adlerian, Jungian, Behavioral, and so forth, with little in the way of in-depth and extensive readings and training for treating any of the specific human problems listed. Psychologists may argue that this problem is now remedied by almost all fifty states requiring yearly continuing education courses in order to maintain licensure. However, the rebuttal consists of two parts. The first involves the development of mind sets or rather a fixed way of looking at things, which is often engrained during the first years of training. Indeed, it is this very mindset that continues to permeate the dogged adherence to an arcane and ineffective training model in the first place. Festinger (1977) aptly calls this *effort justification,* which means if one exerts considerable effort into learning a skill, then one is going to cling tenaciously to what he or she has learned, excluding any information that may contradict their ingrained paradigm. Whether or not such mindsets can be altered with weekend or online abbreviated postdoctoral courses is, of course, an empirical question, but common sense observations seems to indicate that the tradition of the old curriculum model is being tenaciously clung to and is therefore most likely responsible for psychology not changing and not adapting to a more productive training curricula. The second part of the rebuttal consists of the idea that abbreviated weekend courses or quickie online courses cannot possibly cover each of the specific life problems with sufficient depth. Thus, the APA accreditation requirements are in dire need of reform, but there seems to be little chance of that happening anytime soon. Thus, doctoral programs are not doing a very good job, which is made apparent by the weak showing of treatment efficacies.

The second glaring problem one may notice is that the most frequent required course is *assessment or psychometrics.* Why? We have already looked at the assessment problem, and as Walter Mischel (1996) points out in an astute and scholarly fashion, we are doing very poorly at predicting behaviors in specific settings, and we are not very good at matching assessment to diagnosis, a diagnostic system that is greatly in need of reconceptualization anyway. Why is the most frequently course offered consisting of invalid and unreliable misinformation and disinformation? The argument that it is *useful information* as part of the evaluation process is absolutely wrong. How can wrong information be useful? In fact, if such information is used in the courts for custody hearings, criminal culpability, and so forth, then it is downright dangerous (Faust, Anderer, and Ziskin, 2001; revision in press). This practice is unconscionable.

A third problem seems to be the extreme emphasis on statistic and research methodology. Is this a useful use of graduate school training time sufficient time for learning to treat specific human problems for which we identified forty-one different types of problems? Cognitive/behavioral treatments offer fairly well-researched concepts and methods for dealing with many of these problems, and the self-help book market is replete with lots of valuable material for dealing with these same problems. This would consume every spare minute for the trainee. Research courses consume too much time and should be electives for those students who know that they wish to be academician researchers. Medical students do not do spend time studying research. They are exclusively devoted to mastering treatments for clinical problems. The argument may be made that the doctorate of psychology degree remedies this excessive emphasis on research. No, it does not! Those programs are included in these summary tables and indicate that their courses are the same as for the doctor of philosophy programs. It does eliminate the dissertation, but still too much time is spent on research courses.

An overview of the course offerings, whether core, specialty, or elective, reveals that they have little to do with the understanding and amelioration of specific human problems. They are filled with abstraction, philosophical psychology, research, and so forth. In other words, they are collectively a more in-depth study of *introductory psychology*. Again, this is analogous to a medical student taking and retaking all of his introductory biology courses. Psychology must make up its mind whether its doctoral training is academically oriented, which seems to fulfill the needs of only 15 percent of those taking the clinical degree or whether it is a practicing degree, which seems to be the needs of 85 percent of its students (Zimbardo, Weber, and Johnson, 2000). The discipline must be separated. Time does not permit continuing the tradition of trying to do both at the time.

It is unethical to continue this practice (Hodgson, 2007 in a personal communication, August 29, 2007) because we are dealing with people's lives. When they come to us, they are in pain and/or in need, and yet we are mostly unqualified to handle whatever the presenting problem may be. When we testify in the courts, again, we are lacking the requisite training to make declarations and reports of bogus findings that will affect people's lives. In most states, clinical psychologists are required to take ethics courses in order to maintain their licenses, and yet they practice unethically on a daily basis. Worst of all, no one seems to *get it.*

It is only in the third cluster of courses that we begin to see some evidence of problem-based courses. However, the numbers are discouraging. Only forty-four schools, 38 percent, offer specialty courses in family/marital therapy. This is unconscionable and unacceptable. How can we release clinicians, most of whom have never had in-depth training in marital counseling techniques? Is it any wonder that marriage counseling fails two-thirds of the time? Only forty-three programs, 38 percent, have training in adolescent and child therapy. Is it, therefore, any wonder that we have to increasingly rely on psychiatric drugs with childhood and adolescent disorders? Two-thirds of us are clueless about what it takes to effectively use psychosocial techniques to ameliorate their problems. In other words, most psychologists do not know what they are doing.

We are playing an increasing role in the criminal court system (Dawes, 1994; Dershowitz, 1994; Hagen, 1997), and yet only eight schools, 7 percent, offer forensics courses, and much of them are filled with misinformation with an emphasis on psychological assessment (Faust et al., 2001). The FBI had to develop its own diagnostic system (Douglas, Burgess, Burgess, and Ressler, 1997) to help categorize, profile, and understand criminal conduct because psychology has almost completely neglected this very important arena. It is the discipline of sociology that adopted criminal justice; psychology dropped the ball. Nine programs have courses in law, psychology, and policy, which is again another 7 percent. Only four programs, 3.5 percent, have courses in youth and violence. This is inadequate. This is unacceptable. Crimes, gangs, and drugs are growing problems that are consuming the fabric of this country, and psychology seems to fail to take notice. Every jail and every prison has either staff psychologists or consulting psychologists, and yet few doctoral programs have any training. Research needs to be done to explore what it is that the *shrinks* are doing in these institutions. Certainly, most of them are unprepared and unqualified to deal with the criminal mentality (Samenow, 2007).

Only thirty-two programs, 28 percent, have courses in behavior therapy, which is one of the few therapeutic modalities that are built on a foundation of empirical evidence. Is it any wonder that the treatment efficacy rates with ADD/ADHD is 44 percent (NIH report, 1998), 20 percent with ODD (Flick, 2004), and about 0 percent with delinquents (Samenow, 2004)? Is it any wonder that the popular behavioral treatment approaches are poorly designed and that theoretically they should not work, and realistically they do not (Stein, 2004)?

Only forty-nine programs, 43 percent, offer ethnic and minority issues courses. Do we give lip service to diversity? Are we going to remedy this situation, or are we going to continue teaching more sensation and perception courses?

The Boulder model (Wedding and Mengel, 2004) has been dominating training practices for over seventy years, which emphasizes the course content covered in the tables. It does not work. It is broken. It needs to be fixed. We need to recognize this as fact. The matrix model of Snyder and

Elliott (2005) perpetuates the same old same old. Close examination of the model seems to indicate that it is not very different than the Boulder model. This model also fails to focus on specific human problems. Is the problem that psychology professors stick to tradition because it is easier than doing the enormous work that would be necessary to develop expertise in even one specific human problem? Is it that psychology professors stay fixed in their comfort zones rather than investing long hours, hard work, and even anxiety in order to develop expertise in specific problems? Is this attachment to old dogma the result of Festinger's (1977) *effort justification*, where they enormous effort and work that it took to make it through graduate school has locked psychologists into a mindset from which they cannot extricate themselves?

Medical schools are constantly updating what they teach. New findings must be incorporated into their course content. Medical professors must stay current. Why are psychology professors not doing the same? Clinical psychology, on the one hand, seems to aspire to the medical model, but on the other hand, it refuses to relinquish the old to make way for the new. There is a wealth of literature for almost all the topics previously mentioned, and yet few clinical psychology students are doing required readings in most of the topics, and of course, their professors, out of ignorance, laziness, or addiction to dogma, are not requiring such in-depth reading.

A look at one problem immediately makes it apparent how much the clinician needs to know. Child sexual abuse usually does not involve only the abuse itself. Abuse does not occur in a vacuum. The clinician needs to be familiar with all the other potential problems that surround such abuse (Sgori, 1982). Let us say, for pedagogical purposes, that the father is the abuser, which occurs in the majority of cases. What is the mother's role? What is the likelihood that she has always known it is going on? What help does she need? What about the abusers control of the family? What about the secrecy that all members of the family must maintain? How does secrecy affect a child's peer relationships? What does an abused child do with precocious sexual knowledge? How does it affect a child's behavior in school? What effects accrue when human services, the police, and the courts intervene? Are there treatments for the abusers that are effective? (No!) What does the child experience if he/she reveals what has been going on? What role can the therapist play in helping the child deal with making revelations and possible guilt feelings for the breakup of the family? One can go on and on, but the point is obvious. In this problem alone, the therapist must have a vast amount of knowledge if he is to help all members of the family, and the sad part is that courses in this topic are mostly absent in the graduate training programs. Nay instead, we waste precious time on invalid assessment courses, on endless statistics and research methodology courses, on theoretical falderal, on studying systems of treatment that do not work, and on courses that are mere repetitions of introductory psychology.

Recently, Stein (the author) introduced a proposal for a new course in his department for the *Psychology of Terrorism and Homeland Security*. It took two and one half years of difficult and meticulous preparation to make ready for teaching the course. Countless hours were spent reading. Countless hours were spent reviewing media materials. The author had the good fortune of having police security clearance and therefore could attend private government meetings on terrorism and homeland security. Wherever possible, he took courses at police training academies. Preparations were difficult and sometimes even painful. Staying current on the topic requires even more diligence. But this is what it will take for graduate professors to develop expertise in most of the human problem issues. Thus far, few seem willing to invest the time and energy in order to make the transition in to modernizing graduate clinical training. It is so much easier to stay in the comfort zone and maintain tradition.

We will help humans with specific human problems when we begin learning what those problems are and what it takes to ameliorate them. It may turn out that even if course content were modernized into the twenty-first century that treatment efficacy rates do not improve simply because humans stubbornly refuse to change, but this is an empirical question that will not be answered until psychology itself changes. We are not, as the introductory texts would have us believe, *scientific practitioners.* We are practitioners of unadulterated *rubbish!*

BIBLIOGRAPHY

Anastasi, A. (1988). *Psychological Testing.* New York: Macmillan Publishing Company.

Bandura, A. (1969). *Principles of Behavior Modification.* Lanham, MD: Holt, Rinehart, and Winston.

Barlow, D. and Durand, V. W. (2006). *Abnormal Psychology: An Integrative Approach.*

New York: Brooks/Cole Publishing Company.

Barlow, D., Leitenberg, H., and Steinbook, R. M. (1969). "Experimental Control of Sexual Deviation through Manipulation of the Noxious Scene in Covert Sensitization." *J. Abnormal Psychology,* 1969, 74, 596-601.

Beck, A. (1961). "A Systematic Investigation of Depression." *Comprehensive Psychiatry,* 2, 163-170.

Beck, A. (1979). *Cognitive Therapy and the Emotional Disorders.* New York: Meridian Books.

Becker, W. C., Engelmann, S., and Thomas, D. R. (1971). *Teaching: A Course in Applied Psychology.* Chicago, IL: Science Research Associates, Inc.

Breggin, P. (2002). *The Ritalin Fact Book: What Your Doctor Won't Tell You About ADHD and Stimulant Drugs.* Cambridge, MA: Perseus Publishing.

Dawes, R. M. (1994). *House of Cards: Psychology and Psychotherapy Built on Myth.* New York: The Free Press.

Davison, G. C. and Neale, J. M. (1994). *Abnormal Psychology.* New York: John Wiley and Sons.

Dershowitz, A. (1994). *The Abuse Excuse: And Other Cop-Outs, Sob Stories, and Evasions of Responsibility.* New York: Little, Brown and Company.

Dineen, T. (2000). *Manufacturing Victims: What the Psychology Industry Is Doing to People.* New York: Robert Davies Multimedia Publishing.

Douglas, J., Burgess, A., Burgess, A. G., and Ressler, R. (1997). *Crime Classification Manual: A Standard System for Investigating and Classifying Violent Crimes.* San Francisco: CA: Jossey-Bass Publishers.

Ellis, A. and Harper, R. A. (1975). *A New Guide to Rational Living.* Englewood Cliffs, NJ: Prentice Hall.

Eysenck, H. J. (1952). "The Effects of Psychotherapy: An Evaluation." *Journal of Consulting Psychology, 16,* 319-324.

Eysenck, H. J. (1961). "The Effects of Psychotherapy." In H. J. Eysenck (Ed.), *Handbood of Abnormal Psychology: An Experimental Approach.* New York: Basic Books, Pp. 697-725.

Faust, D., Anderer, D., and Ziskin, J. (2001). *Ziskin's Coping with Psychological Testimony.* Cambridge, MA: Oxford University Press.

Faust, D., Anderer, D., and Ziskin, J. (2001). *Ziskin's Coping with Psychological Testimony.* Cambridge, MA: Oxford University Press.

Festinger, L. (1977). *Leon Festinger.* In David Cohen, *Psychologists on Psychology.* New York: Taplinger Publishers. (pp. 262-266)

Flick, G. L. (2004). *How To Reach and Teach Teenagers with ADHD: A Step-By-Step Guide to Overcome Difficult Behavior at School and at Home.* West Nyack, NY: The Center for Applied Research in Education.

Hagen, M. A. (1997). *Whores of the Court: The Fraud of Psychiatric Testimony and the Rape of American Justice.* New York: HarperCollins Publishers.

Hall, C. S. and Lindzey, G. L. (1957). *Theories of Personality.* New York: John Wiley and Sons.

Kanfer, F. and Phillips, J. S. (1970). *Learning Foundations of Behavior Therapy.* New York: John Wiley and Sons, Inc.

Kendall, P. C. and Hollon, S. D. (1981). *Assessment Strategies for Cognitive-Behavioral Interventions.* New York: Academic Press.

Lilienfeld, S. O., Lynn, S. J., and Lohr, J. M. (2003) (Eds). *Science and Pseudoscience in Clinical Psychology.* New York: The Guilford Press.

Lilienfeld, S. O., Wood, J. M., and Garb, H. N. (2000). "The Scientific Status of Projective Techniques." *Psychological Science in the Public Interest, 1,* 27-66.

Lilienfeld, S. O., Wood, J. M., and Garb, H. N. (2001a, May). What's Wrong with This Picture? *Scientific American, 284(5),* 80-87.

Lipsey, M. W. and Wison, D. B. (1993). "The Efficacy of Psychological, Educational, and Behavioral Treatment: Confirmation from Meta-Analysis. *American Psychologist,* Vol. 48(12), pp. 1181-1209.

Lorandos, D. and Campbell, T. W. (2005). *Benchbook in the Behavioral Sciences.* Durham, NC: Carolina Academic Press.

Maultsby, M. C. (1984). *Rational Behavioral Therapy.* Englewood Ciffs, NJ: Prentice Hall.

McGraw, P. (2000). *Relationship Rescue: A Seven-Step Strategy for Reconnecting with Your Partner.* New York: Hyperion.

Meichenbaum, D. (1977). *Cognitive-Behavioral Therapy.* New York: Plenum Press.

Mischel. W. (1996). *Personality and Assessment.* Mahwah, NJ: Lawrence Erlbaum Associates, Publishers.

Mosby's 2008 Drug Guide. St. Louis, MO: Elesvier.

National Institute of Health Conference, 1998, in Bethesda, MD.

Papolos, D. and Papolos, J. (2002). *The Bipolar Child: The Definitive and Reassuring Guide to Childhood's Most Misunderstood Disorder.* New York: Broadway Books.

Patterson, G. R. (1971). *Families: Applications of Social Learning Theory to Modern Life.* Chicago, IL: Science Research Associates, Inc.

Peele, S. (1995). *Diseasing of America: How We Allowed Recovery Zealots and the Treatment Industry to Convince Us We Are Out of Control.* San Francisco, CA: Jossey-Bass Publishers.

Rossi. P. and Wright, J. D. (1984). Evaluation Research and Assessment. *Annual Review of Sociology,* volume (10), 331-352.

Samenow, S. (2004*). Inside the Criminal Mind.* New York: Crown Business.

Santrock, J. W., Minnett, A. M., and Campbell, B. D. (1994). *The Authoritative Guide to Self-Help Books.* New York: The Guilford Press.

Sgori, S. (1982). *Handbook of Clinical Intervention in Child Sexual Abuse.* New York: The Free Press.

Stein, D. B. (2001a). *Ritalin Is Not the Answer: A Drug-Free, Practical Program for Children Diagnosed with ADD or ADHD.* Lanham, MD: Wiley, Jossey-Bass, Publishers.

Stein, D. B. (2004). *Stop Medicating/Start Parenting: Real Solutions for Your Problem Teenager.* Lanham, MD: Talylor Publishing.

Stein, D. B. (2001b). (2001). *Unraveling the ADD/ADHD Fiasco: Successful Parenting without Drugs.* Kansas City, MO: Andrews McMeel Publishing.

Snyder, C. R. and Elliott, T. R. (2005). "Twenty-First-Century Graduate Education in Clinical Psychology: A Four-Level Matrix Model." *Journal of Clinical Psychology, 61,* 1033-1054.

Strauss, A. and Lehtinen, L. (1947). *Psychopathology and Education of the Brain-Impaired Child.* New York: Greene & Stratton.

Valenstein, E. S. (1998). *Blaming the Brain: The Truth About Drugs and Mental Health.* New York: The Free Press.

Wedding, D., and Mengel, M. (2004). "Models of Integrated Care in Primary Care Settings." In L. Haas (Ed.). *Handbook of Psychology in Primary Care.* (pp. 47-62). New York: Oxford University Press.

Wilson, J. W. (2002). *The Marriage Problem: How Our Culture Has Weakened Families.* New York: HarperCollins Publishers.

Wolpe, J. (1958). *Psychotherapy by Reciprocal Inhibition.* San Francisco, CA: Stanford University Press.

Wood. J. M., Nezworski, M. T., Lilienfeld, S. O., and Grab, H. N. (2003). *What's Wrong with the Rorschach?* San Francisico, CA: Wiley, Jossey-Bass.

The Black Borders Of Indianess: The Categorial And Social Incarceration Of A Mixed-Race People

Anjana Mebane-Cruz, Ph.D.
Farmingdale State College, New York

Abstract

The development of race categories and ideologies based on hierarchies of color and blood created particular problems for "mixed" people in the United States. With "whiteness" favored above all else, mixed people often self-identified with the lighter of their ancestors in spite of prohibitive legal sanctions. However, for the children of Africans/African-Americans and American-Indians, the options were more limited, and their position within American society was far more luminal. Most who would now fall into the unofficial category popularly known as "Black Indians" identified themselves as either only Indian or only Black. Because of particular rules, laws, and practices in the U.S., those who could identify as Indian rarely acknowledged African descent, while those who were categorized as "Black" could seldom officially identify their indigenous roots. By exploring racial categories as a form of incarceration, this paper will give an overview history of some mergers between "Indians" and "Black" people, investigate the idea that race categories are more akin to incarceration than standard ideas of social control, and note the recent disintegration of historical Black-Red alliances in conjunction with the rise of casino gambling and the growth of a unique racism within reservation politics.

Keywords: African-Americans; American-Indians; Black Indians; Cultural Anthropology; Ethics; History and Memory; Identity; Mixed Race; Racism

INTRODUCTION

CONSTRUCTED AND CONTESTED IDENTITIES

Over the past few centuries, various laws and policies have constructed race as a normative category. In the United States, this has created a sociopolitical hierarchy based on race categories with *whiteness,* not only at the top of the chart but promoted as the desired category. While all other categories were subordinate to *white/Caucasian, black/Negro* became the lowest category, and *blackness* became the defining border of all races. This did not happen overnight, and the practical, political reasons that a growing, emerging country would enact certain rules and laws had much to do with economic pragmatism. The enslaved population could be increased without resorting to continual purchasing by first changing the prevailing European-based common laws of inheritance so that the children of enslaved people were born enslaved, despite parentage.[1] First legislated in Virginia, in 1662, these laws also associated race with slavery, specifying that the children of *Negro/mulatto* female slaves would also be slaves. This is significant, not only in breaking with traditionally strict British rules on inheritance through the male lineage but also in specifying one particular group of enslaved people among several, for at that time, American-Indians were also commonly enslaved. Sometimes classified as *mulattos,* American-Indians who could not prove their racial identity were lumped together with African and American blacks, as were the children of lower-class whites who worked with and mingled with the now-socially illegalized blacks.

The second significant and practical aspect of these changing rules and laws had to do with the relationship between the colonies (and later the United States) and the indigenous Indian nations. Simply stated, because the U.S. has treaties with the various Native American groups that date back to the early European invaders, it has been in the interests of the country to have fewer Indians to deal with and thus, fewer obligations to the remaining Indian nations. To that end, U.S. policy has traditionally negated claims of Indian ancestry as well as Indian treaty rights. Furthermore, American-Indians and African-Americans are the only

---

[1]   Act XII, *Laws of Virginia,* December 1662 (Hening, *Statutes at Large,* 2: 170)

two groups in the United States to have had blood quantum regulations legislated and enforced. The rule of hypo-descent or "one drop" rule was applied to African-Americans, first as a means of increasing the enslaved population and later through explicit and tacit—Jim Crow segregation as a tactic of continuing social incarceration. Blood quantum rules for American-Indians followed the incarceration of their nations onto reservations and the division of Indian lands among their conquerors, limiting access to only the descendants of indigenous peoples who could trace their blood lineages to the relatively few Indians listed on federal rolls taken through the Dawes Act of 1887. And although each Indian nation is allowed to decide their own blood quantum requirement for tribal enrollment, the primacy of blood as the definitive way of determining kinship was and is a Western perspective forced upon groups whose traditional means for determining kinship were often based on relationships and alliances, not merely blood. With these rules and other laws, Blacks and Indians—who had been allies for generations—were now separated through opposing categories of blood. *AfraAmerIndians* needed to be able to document close blood ties to names on the Dawes and similar rolls in order to be considered Indians, and recognized Indians had to distance themselves from their Black allies and relatives if they wished to maintain any claims to Indian identity, ancestral lands, and some slight sense of autonomy. Both being at the bottom of the U.S. economy and social scale, the two groups became competitors, first in avoidance of the state's lash and then for the crumbs of dignity and economic promise that the government offered.

Each state had its own definition for "Black," but each found it necessary to define this particular category, sometimes—as in the case of Oklahoma—making *whiteness* everything not defined as *Black* (López 1996; 119-120). Interestingly, Virginia "defined Blacks as those in whom there was "ascertainable any Negro blood" with not more than one-sixteenth Native American ancestry." (López 1996: 120) Lopez continues:

"The very practice of legally defining Black identity demonstrates the social, rather than natural, basis of race. Moreover, these competing definitions demonstrate that the many laws that discriminated on the basis of race more often than not defined and thus helped to create the categories they claimed only to elucidate. In defining Black and White, statutory and case law assisted in fashioning the racial significance that by themselves drops of blood, ascertainable amounts, and fractions never could have. In the name of racially regulating behavior, laws *created* racial identities." [Lopez, 1996: 120]

Furthermore, these laws explicate Bruno Latour's contention that modern classifications that fixate on polarities of *pure* and *impure* must, inevitably, by their nature, create hybridity as well. [2](Latour 2000) The very idea of race is tied to notions of biological difference and inherent superiority and inferiority. These notions continue despite our scientific repudiation of the validity of such notions. (See Marks, 1995, 2011 and Goodman, 1996, 2006) We still live in a society that clings to concepts of racial purity despite the ties these ideas have to Eugenics, Nazis, and other genocides and ethnocides around the world and our proclaimed abhorrence of such philosophies. Inherent within notions of purity are notions of superiority and inferiority that negate our professed desire for a society based on equality, fairness, or equal "justice for all."[3]

Because the category of the dominant culture has been the most privileged and normalized, members of the subdominant groups compete not only against the dominant group but most particularly against one another. Race is not a neutral designation, and with each designation, limits of public and social agency were practiced and written into law. The racisms that developed have served to essentialize race and foster ideas about each group that have become normalized and accepted almost universally. With legally imposed rules regarding education, housing, travel, marriage, suffrage, etc., for each group, former allies found themselves competing for resources and respect. Divided in these ways and educated by the dominant culture, mutual histories were mostly lost and marginalized when remembered. By the twentieth century, the once-possible cooperation between Blacks and Indians had been undermined

---

[2]   In this work, Latour's larger framework of inquiry includes the scientific approach, and in so doing, he notes the modern separation of human endeavor/culture from Nature and the natural world. Similarly, there is a modern tendency—perhaps promoted along with African slavery and colonization—to treat race difference as though it was species difference and not merely a shorthand for superficial phenotype or culture variation.

[3]

or eliminated, and the historical facts of two centuries of mutual servitude and alliances had been forgotten or downplayed in order to privilege one or the other group in efforts to promote short term benefits.

In March 2007, the Cherokee Nation, following a growing pattern among Native American tribal nations, expelled two thousand eight hundred descendants of African slaves from the Nation. The vast majority of these people, like their ancestors, had lived as Cherokee citizens since before the infamous *Trail of Tears*, mixing with other Cherokees and neighboring Native Americans and serving the nation, not only as slaves but as valued members of that society.

In the same year, the Narragansett of Rhode Island continued what was becoming a trend, as had thirteen California tribes. This death knell in *AfraAmerIndian* relations had been rung when, in 2002, the Oklahoma Seminoles determined not to include the Seminole Freedmen—who had previously been listed as members of the Seminole tribes—when receiving the benefits of a fifty-six-million-dollar suit. When the Freedmen tried to bring suit against the Seminole in 2002, the U.S. government refused to allow the Freedmen to sue for inclusion without the approval of the Seminole Nation, thus upholding the disenfranchisement of this tiny nation within a nation within a nation. [4]

This was a particularly cruel blow to the Seminole Freedmen whose history and culture are inextricably bound to the rest of the Seminole people. The conglomeration of renegades who banded together and fought against U.S. imperialism and encroachment from the late seventeenth to eighteenth centuries eventually became known as

---

[4]   The Cherokee Freedmen were reinstated as citizens of the Cherokee Nation by the Cherokee Nation Tribal Courts on May 15, 2007, pending appeals in the Cherokee Nation Courts and Federal Court. However, in August 2007, the BIA approved the Cherokee Nation's right to modify their constitution without approval from the Department of the Interior. The case heard in the U.S. Court of Appeals in May 2008, where the Freedmen's rights were again upheld. However, the Cherokee Nation launched an appeal to the Cherokee Nation District Court which also upheld the Freedmen rights in 2011. The Cherokee Nation has announced that it plans to appeal this decision as well. Several related cases are outstanding in U.S. federal courts.

Seminole[5] was composed of escaped slaves, free persons of color, Creek, Miccosukee, Hitichi, and Yamasee Indians. The Africans/ *AfraAmerIndians* accepted as Seminoles were renowned for their fighting abilities and advanced farming skills and were valuable members of the Native American resistance and later rebuilding. Thus, these Freedmen trace their roots not only through slavery but as allies against Euro-American expansionism for the better part of a century. Their disenrollment was a flagrant denial of shared histories and culture, but most significantly for many, it also served as another important marker indicating the further submission of Native American sovereignty to federal oversight and their native acceptance of racist, eugenics based metastructures inherent in federal regulations and state procedures.

In *Discipline and Punish*, Foucalt opens the chapter, "The Gentle Way in Punishment," by saying, "The art of punishing, then, must rest on a whole technology of representation."[6] At least in part, he refers to the many substructures that cause us to think of punishment in particular ways and which are created through ideology, coercion, and implication, as well as the threat of incarceration and other physical threats. Judgment—both social and legal—is followed by punishment—both psychic and physical—including the shame and loss brought to families and others associated with the criminalized person or group. Our ability to wield these powers is directly tied to our recognition that we are interdependent and rely on the goodwill of our neighbors as well as our own ability to make our way in the world without running afoul of the systems we have inherited and support, with or without our conscious consent.

---

[5]   A bastardization of the Spanish *cimarrón* and Creek *simanóoli*, meaning "runaway." (Martin & Mauldin, 2004)

[6]   Discipline and Punish The Birth of the Prison, Michel Foucault [1975] 1979; Vintage Books, New York; 104
      In this benchmark case, Mildred-a Black woman, and John-a White man-Loving were prosecuted in Virginia for breaking the antimisegenation laws. Sentenced to a year in jail, they agreed to leave the State rather than serve the jail term. In 1963 they challenged the Virginia laws and the U.S. Supreme Court ruled that the Virginia laws were unconstitutional and violated both Due Process and Equal Protection Clauses of the 14th Amendment.

By the time of the 1958 *Loving v. Virginia* 4decision, the punishment for interracial marriage still included fines, possible incarceration, and the expulsion of the couple from the state for a period of twenty-five years. For the average person, these were harsh punishments that few could afford, perhaps most particularly forced exile and separation from kin, kith, and familiar places. The threat of physical harm was not far removed for such couples or their relatives who would—for the nonwhite family— be suspected of being "uppity" and a threat to white purity; and for the white family, of having produced a "race traitor" and perhaps themselves being tainted with *blackness.*

Blackness continued to be seen and *treated* as inherently problematic and as an inferior state of being, and the containment of the problem group was manifested through physical separation of housing and all levels of social interaction. While very small children in rural areas might be allowed to play together, all such activities ended before puberty, and acts of psychological damage were performed to ensure that children of different races knew their place in the larger society and particularly that Black children knew that their place was always below that of White people of any class or station. Whites who did not adhere to these sanctions were generally punished through shaming and ostracism, while Blacks were more often physically assaulted or even murdered, within or outside of the law. Agency at all levels, including access to housing; education, travel, work, and entertainment, were all regulated according to race, with Blacks at the very bottom of the hierarchy.

So although there were generally no laws dealing directly with *miscegenation* between peoples of color and the general laws were seldom clear, it was obvious to everyone that *blackness* was the one immutable border between the races, the one category that was perpetually fixed and made solid despite the obvious flaws in the logic. To be Black was to be incarcerated within the one category without apparent fluidity or social cachet. It was, both in the perception and reality of most Americans, a form of punishment and incarceration, all rolled into one. Although there were any number of people within the category who wore it with pride and a healthy sense of identity, on the ground and in daily reality, it was still the category associated with nonnegotiable limitations and suffering. To move from any other category to *Black* was to have been tried and found guilty, and the punishment for that taint meant exclusion from safety, security, and the lure of the entitlements of *whiteness* as a possibility for all time. No amount of mixing could ever erase the socially constructed "horror" of having African ancestry among American Whites. This was well understood by every other group of "lesser whites" and indigenous peoples that were paying attention or hoped for inclusion into mainstream America, *"passing"* notwithstanding.

Conversely, nonwhites and "social coloreds"—immigrants from countries other than England and a very few other western European nations—sought to "whiten" themselves through marriage and by entering the middle class through education and position. (See Berger, 1999; Brodkin 1998; Ignatiev, 1995; Goldberg 1993; Roediger, 1991) In the United States, the separation of classes seems obvious, but race complicates the matter and prevents neat lines from being drawn. In theory, at least since legal changes were made in the 1960s, people of color could enter the upper classes. In terms of income, some few have. However, the ranks of those who own/control the means of producing wealth remain solidly white—if you don't count certain *foreign* interests. And even if foreign interested are considered, despite phenotype or lineage, major allies to the U.S. are categorized by the U.S. as "white" and allotted the privileges and agency that *whiteness* confers within U.S. borders. [7]

Within the communities of color, the pressure to whiten led to many forms of self-policing, shaming, and punishment, including the development of a hierarchy and aesthetic that placed those with European features higher on the scale than any other phenotype. Again, features and behaviors considered to be more African-like were at the lowest point

---

[7]   Foreign nationals who are of similar classes in their own countries are always issued American travel visas/passports that identify them as being racially "white" in order to prevent any possible exposure to the way that citizens of color might be mistreated. Of course, at the levels that such people travel, this is unlikely, but their official status in the US reflects their worth rather than bloodlines.

on the scale and created a base border by which every group—including African Americans—would test and rate themselves.[8]

Native Americans, who had been under siege since Columbus stumbled onto their shores, were particularly vulnerable in many ways, especially the eastern tribes which had been severally decimated for so long, suffering through the long period of the Removals to western territories and the Caribbean. The southern tribes were dealt a harsh blow when Thomas Jefferson decreed that Virginia Indians were mixed with Blacks and therefore not Indians, and later, when the category of Indian was legally removed, an act now considered "documentary genocide" by most Native Americans[9]. As William Loren Katz (1986) aptly states, "Jefferson, a founding father of America, established the 'you don't look Indian' precedent when he decided that there was 'more negro than Indian blood' among the Mattaponies of his home state Virginia" and most importantly, because Jefferson problematized the mixture, conveniently insisting that Virginian Indians had ceased to exist *because* of their "Negro" blood. Although the rule of hypo-descent—more commonly referred to as the "one drop rule"—had not been written into law at the time, it was codified in tradition throughout the U.S., causing members of various nations to be displaced from their lands and eventually removed from tribal ranks and memory. For those remaining within the tribes, it became crucial to deny any connection to *blackness* and for those who recognized their own mixed heritage, to discriminate against Blacks and distance themselves as much as possible. Although it's seldom discussed outside of the clans, this has been a common practice among the Eastern tribes, particularly since the Jim Crow era. Again, *blackness* is reified as the defining border, crossed only at the peril of the death of all other cultural and legal identities.

---

[8] The recognition of this important social and psychological development within communities of color would play an important role in the landmark 1955 case, *Brown vs. Board of Education* decision when it was shown through psychological testing that Black children felt inferior to Whites and would not receive an equal education under the terms of segregation.

[9] An accessible and excellent exposition of this situation was written by J. David Smith in his 1993, *The Eugenic Assault on America.*

Phillip J. DeLoria takes on the history of White Americans appropriating native identities in his 1998 work, *Playing Indian*, but in an earlier, important article, "The Tribe Called Wannabee: Playing Indian in America and Europe" (1988), Rayna Green touched on Black-Indian relations but unfortunately, accepted the dominant society's two rules for discourse on the subject: ignore it or dismiss it as Black "escapism." Even while acknowledging that relations between Blacks and Indians have been ignored, she goes on to dismiss claims of authenticity by AfraAmerIndians, stating that these were fantasies "connecting to a world that allows them to be first, to be other than Black, other than white, *other than victims who did not fight their enslavement.*" (p. 48; emphasis mine) With this statement, Green follows in the footsteps of Vine DeLoria who, in his famous work, "Custer Died for Your Sins," stated, "It is fortunate that we were never slaves; we gave up land instead of life and labor. Because the Negro labored, he was considered a draft animal."

It was amazing that this educated and savvy writer published this statement, but what is more disturbing than what might have been DeLoria's ignorance is that fact that the statement has, by and large, gone unchallenged, even in the face of all the historical evidence of Black revolts, insurrections, and myriad forms of resistance, *including* alliances with indigenous Americans. His words also fly in the face of the known and documented history of American-Indian slavery that started with Columbus and which did not end even when Africans were brought to the Americas. First Nations peoples and Africans labored together, resisted together, and in all other ways mixed, as surely as did other groups that lived and worked together.

No, the idea of the African and the African-American is firmly linked in the minds of most Americans of *any* ethnicity or cultural background with the conditions of slavery, and as in other forms of incarceration, the parties within the category are considered guilty and as in other forms of incarceration; even if new evidence is presented, it does not guarantee that the convicted party will be released from prison. The metastructures of our society, through legal precedence and social tradition, continue to normalize notions of white supremacy and racism and through the denial of BIA benefits to punish Native American nations that have attempted to maintain autonomy and adhere to their own traditionally more equitable methods for dealing with "insider-outsider" relations. Although it is a common traditional Indian practice to categorize people as being *Indians* or *non-Indians*—with *Indian* being defined as those who live the life and generally have blood or historical ties to the group—Indian perceptions and practices have been heavily influenced by the dominant culture and its racial and other hierarchies, often to the exclusion of even those cultural Indians who are of African descent. (See Naylor, 2006; Pratt, 2007, also Naylor-Ojurongbe, McMullen, and Welburn, 2002)

Add to this scenario the lure of casino money, and perhaps we begin to understand the disenrollment process that has come to dominate *AfraAmerIndian* relations with the tribes. Indian nations distribute the revenues from their casinos to all members of the tribe. When first started, casino revenues were seen as the way to uplift Native communities that were below the national poverty line and plagued with all the societal ills that accompany deprivation. As the casinos became more popular, tribes were faced with a sudden increase in applicants for tribal enrollment and were forced, once again, to reconsider their ideas about tribal identity as well as what would be acceptable to their state and federal governments since, until recently, state approval was sought by tribes seeking gaming licensing. While federal statutes claim[10] that individual tribes decide their own blood quantum and other requirements for enrollment, in fact, the tribes which have been historically seen by the federal government—going back to Jefferson—as being compromised with African blood have been denied full recognition despite their ability to show continuity of placement, language, or other criteria for federal enrollment. There has been only one exception when, in 2010, with President Obama's support, the Shinnecock Nation's decades old appeal was finally won.[11]

The problem has obviously not been one of *mixing* but rather of which ingredients are being mixed. On one level, *mixing* implies impurity and danger, concepts embedded in the dichotomy of the American psyche,

---

[10] Department of the Interior: Bureau of Indian Affairs 25 CRF Part 70 RIN 1076-AD98 Certificate of Degree of Indian or Alaska Native Blood

[11] The Shinnecock first applied for federal recognition in 1978. In this 2009, the sitting Governor of New York brought the petition to President Obama's attention, a historic first in these matters.

inherited and nourished since before the *Puritan* pilgrims landed. But perhaps the deeper aspect of *mixing* that creates a problem in our type of society and for the colonized folk within it is that *mixing* defies the rigorous training—the discipline, according to Foucault—that we think we need in order to maintain control and which of course must always elude since a system based on notions of purity creates then its own counterpoint of impurity. (See Latour, 1993)

Foucault notes the training within such hierarchies and the system of rewards and punishments that are intrinsic to the training period. He notes the way in which "mental patients and delinquents" (Foucault, p. 192) are categorized through "ritual and scientific" examination which, while individualizing, also marginalizes the individual and in some sense, prepares her for the *proper* discipline and punishment. So too does the training of citizens categorized within a constructed hierarchy of racist categories prepare them for the disciplines, incentives, and punishments associated with their particular category. It is the Eastern tribes who have been made explicit examples in this ongoing culture-identity war, while their former allies and relatives in Africa-America have been silenced on the subject. A carefully constructed set of perceptions denies the reality of "mixed" identities as well as the standing of Blacks who might have something to say but are habitually denied the right to speak authoritatively.

American-Indian writer, Craig Womack,[12] recently noted the absence of Native characters in the works of most African-American fiction authors, citing Toni Morrison in particular for her "disappearing Indians" in the 1998 novel, *Paradise,* in his talk, "Toni Morrison's Novels: American-Indian Presence or Absence?" He expresses ambiguity in criticizing Morrison, admitting to certain happiness in finding *any* Indian characters in the works of a non-Indian writer. Yet with notable exceptions such as Dorris (1987) and Forbes (1995), Blacks are absent from Indian literature; and importantly, this is not problematized! Because the perception continues that Blacks and Indians are completely separate groups with

---

[12] Associate Professor of English, Emory University, author of 1999's *Red on Red: Native American Literary Separatism* at the Society for the Study of Southern Literature Annual Conference, College of William & Mary, Williamsburg, Va. April, 2008

no real overlap, few writers feel the need to include either group in their visions of American landscape(s). Furthermore, I suspect that in the case of minority writers still struggling to find outlets in U.S. literature, there is a reluctance to take on these particularly complex issues of identity, still fraught with political and social danger.

So in spite of migrations and new routes, we remain rooted in the boxes of identity and the limits of category forged by our captors. Each group has played a part in the larger betrayals of the values of their ancestral communities; Blacks became *Indian Fighters* and homesteaders on Indian lands, sometimes taking on the same attitudes toward Native peoples as their Euro-American counterparts. While African-Americans are recognized as being subject to criminalization tactics, the same process is used against Indigenous Americans[11] but seldom discussed[13] *Native* peoples did not stand up to the enrollment process under Dawes and later used these shameful rules to disinherit and disown their *Black/Native* kin and allies. Casino money and the desire to become federally enrolled have led some First Nations groups to reinterpret their histories and alliances in order to become "players" in their home states and, in effect, buy into the existing racist power structure. And of course, there is the pervasive ignorance by both groups to the intricacies of their shared histories and connections.

Many have been weighing the question of sovereignty and the rights of tribal nations to decide their criteria for enrollment, and a few have even pondered the risks of identity and culture loss in the process of modernizing and attempting to bring benefits to their people, but I would like to trouble the waters further. For the various peoples who fall within and between the categories of *Black* or *Indian*, the question has to be: If we continue to deny and dissolve our alliances and to fashion ourselves through the eyes of our captors, who do we become, and how will we be recognized by the ancestors and the generations? In other words, what are the limits of *identity* and *culture*? Are we truly able to maintain core cultural bits that allow us to consider ourselves part of whichever group we identified with, or is this just a form of denial? These are key questions for anthropologists and for the folk that we work with, and they are

---

13

questions that have often been addressed in ways that limited the voice and input of the various "natives" that anthropologists considered *their* subjects. But hundreds of years later, indigenous peoples must consider these questions in all their complexities and ask at what point does a group become so compromised by their external situation that they are no longer recognizable to themselves in terms of the values and beliefs that were the locus of identity for the earlier people that embodied or created the "prototype" or "template" for the culture? Similarly, is it not a form of racism to continue to lock the various *natives* of the world into cultural prisons of identity as determined by Europeans during colonialism? All peoples and cultures change over time, but they key difference is that before colonialism, these changes and identity markers were determined to a much greater degree by the peoples themselves.

AfraAmerIndians exist as surely as other perceived "mixed" groups or even groups we like to think of as being more homogeneous. Some questions then are: How shall they be recognized, and what part does official policy have in a process of recognition or denial? Furthermore, can groups still regulated by the federal government really go against general government policies on issues that bring into question their own legitimacy as "protected" entities? And of course, there is the original question of how we categorize and thus contain the increasingly complex groups of people in the postmodern globalized world. While some call for DNA testing, this is a more complex proposition than most realize and, to be done "fairly," would require both X and Y chromosome testing. Furthermore, despite the growing popularity of such tests, the information they provide at this time is limited and still open to interpretation. Perhaps most disturbing for many, the results of such tests could force the reclassification of a majority of people, including many now categorized as White. If we use this information to eliminate race categories in the U.S., we're still left with the determination of identity in a way that recognizes that our history and its continuing affects should not allow us to disregard the disparities between the White majority and the descendants of its Captured Nations. If we accept the scientific reality that the DNA of all human groups is traceable to sub-Saharan African origins, then we have to look at culture difference in order to maintain the types of boundaries to which we seem wed as a society. And if we accept culture as the border, then it must be determined at which point in history can any culture be definitively defined, a prospect that can only remain contested.

REFERENCES

Berger, Maurice (1999)*White Lies: Race and the Myths of Whiteness*: New York: Farrar, Straus, Giroux

Brodkin, Karen (1998) *How Jews Became White Folks and What That Says About Race in America*. New Jersey: Rutgers University Press

Deloria, Phillip J (1998) *Playing Indian*. New Haven, Yale University Press

Deloria, Vine, Jr.91988) *Custer Died for Your Sins: An Indian Manifesto.* Norman & London: University of Oklahoma

Dorris, Michael (1987) *A Yellow Raft in Blue Water*. New York: Henry Holt & Co.

Forbes, Jack D. (1993) [88] *Africans and Native Americans: The Language of Race and the Evolution of Red-Black Peoples*. Champaign: University of Illinois Illini Books

Foucault, Michel (1979) [75] *Discipline and Punishment: The Birth of the Prison*, New York: Random House

Goldberg, David Theo (1993) *Racist Culture: Philosophy and the Politics of Meaning.* Oxford, U.K., Cambridge, U.S.

Goodman, Alan (2006) *Two Questions About Race.* Social Science Research Council http://raceandgenomics.ssrc.org/Goodman/

Goodman, Alan, and Armelago, George J. (1996) *Race, Racism, and the New Physical Anthropology in Race and Other Misadventures:* Essays in Honor of Ashley Montagu in His Ninetieth Year. Larry T. Reynolds and Leonard Lieberman, eds. pp. 174-182. Maryland: AltaMira Press

Green, Rayn (1988) "The Tribe Called Wannabe: Playing Indian in American and Europe," Folklore 1 (9) pp. 30-35

Hogan, Linda (2001) New York: W.W. Norton Company

Ignatiev, Noel (1995) *How the Irish Became White*. New York, London: Routledge

Katz, William Loren
1986 *Black Indians: A Hidden Heritage*. New York: Antheneum

Latour, Bruno
1993 [91] *We Have Never Been Modern*, Cambridge: Harvard University Press

López, Ian F. Haney
1996 *White by Law: The Legal Construction of Race*, New York and London: New York University Press

Marks, Jonathan
1995 Human Biodiversity: Genes, Race, and History
2011 The Alternative Introduction to Biological Anthropology New York: University of Oxford Press

Martin, Jack B., and Margaret McKane Mauldin
2004 *A Dictionary of Creek/Muskogee*, Lincoln: University of Nebraska Press

McMullen, Ann
2002 *Blood and Culture: Negotiating Race in Twentieth-Century Native New England. In* Confounding the Color Line, James F. Brooks, ed. pp. 261-291, Lincoln and London: University of Nebraska Press

Naylor, Celia E.
2006 *Playing Indian?: The Selection of Radmilla Cody as Miss Navajo Nation 1997-1998.* In *Crossing Waters, Crossing Worlds: The African Diaspora in Indian Country*, Tiya A. Miles and Sharon P. Holland, eds. pp. 224-248, Durham: Duke University Press.

2002 (Naylor-Ojurongbe) *Born and Raised among These People, I Don't Want to Know Any Other: Slaves Acculturation in Nineteenth-Century Indian Territory.* In "Confounding the Color Line: The Indian-Black Experience in North America." James F. Brooks, ed. pp. 161-191, Lincoln and London: University of Nebraska Press.

Pratt, Carla D.
2007 "Loving Indian Style: Maintaining Racial Caste and Tribal Sovereignty through Sexual Assimilation," Wisconsin Law Review Vol. 2007 No. 2, pp. 410-462

Roediger, David
1991 *The Wages of Whiteness: Race and the Making of the American Working Class.* New York, London: Verso

Smith, J., David
1992 *The Eugenic Assault on America: Scenes in Red, White, and Black.* Fairfax: George Mason University Press

Welburn, Ron. 2002 *A Most Secret Identity: Native American Assimilation and Identity Resistance in African America.* In "Confounding the Color Line: The Indian-Black Experience in North America," James F. Brooks, ed. Lincoln and London: University of Nebraska Press

Womack, Craig
2009 *Tribal Paradise Lost, but Where Did It Go? Native Absence in Toni Morrison's Paradise* Studies in American Indian Literatures, Vol. 21, No. 4, Winter 2009
2008 Remarks at the Society for the Study of Southern Literature Annual Conference, College of William and Mary, Williamsburg, Va. April, 2008

Influence of HIV-AIDS Public Enlightenment Campaigns on Adolescents' Sexual Behavior in Nigeria

A.A. Adegoke Obafemi Ph.D Awolowo University,Ile ife, Nigeria
J.E. Fife Virginia State University
B. Pearson Virginia State University

ABSTRACT

This paper assessed the influence of HIV/AIDS public enlightenment campaigns on adolescents' sexual behavior. The interactions of respondents' sex, age, and parent educational status with sexual behaviors were also explored.

Data generated from a survey conducted among 1902 (917 males and 985 females) adolescent students in Ibadan, Nigeria, were analyzed using SPSS at the .05 level of significance. The obtained results revealed that adolescents have been exposed to a variety of HIV/AIDS campaigns. The broadcast media (television and radio) exerted more significant influence on adolescents' sexual behaviors, while the print media exerted greater influence on their knowledge, attitudes, and beliefs about HIV/AIDS. Also, adolescents' knowledge, attitude, and beliefs about HIV/AIDS had significant positive influence on their sexual behaviors.

INTRODUCTION

Throughout history, human beings have been faced with disastrous catastrophes which must be endured in order to survive. Acquired immune deficiency syndrome (AIDS) caused by the human immunodeficiency virus (HIV) remains one of the most incomprehensible disasters for humanity. An estimated number of people living with HIV stood at over 33.3 million at the end of year 2007. Of this figure, 22.5 million are from Sub-Saharan Africa, the region with most affected victims in the global AIDS epidemic. More than three quarters (76%) of all AIDS deaths in 2007 came from Africa, with another 1.7 million cases of newly infected people. (UNAIDS/WHO, 2008).

The last two decades have witnessed quantum of research work on issue on HIV/AIDS. Scientific literature is full of materials with diverse research interests. In the early years of the detection of the disease, some scientists focused on laboratory studies, examining the causative pathogens and conditions associated with human pathological transmission and various sources of agents and routes responsible for the transmission. A significant proportion of researchers have worked on possible solution to the infectious disease, addressing the possibility of developing a vaccine that can be used for inoculation or drug to cure already infected individuals. This has met with little success. Researchers in the social sciences have concentrated on the implications of the disease on the society. Particular emphasis has been on the behavioral adjuncts associated with the disease.

Prominent in this endeavor is the examination of lifestyle of the so-called "risk groups" and other behavioral factors predisposing individuals to contracting the disease. Men having Sex with Men (MSM), Prostitutes, Commercial Sex Workers (CSW), and Intravenous Drug Users (IDUs) were the first target risk groups identified for HIV/AIDS. Emphasis has gradually been shifted to the populace at large, having noted that it is not individuals labelled as "at risk," but one's lifestyle constitutes a major determinant factor in HIV/AIDS prevention.

Generally, it is believed that the media is a powerful and influential means of educating the public on many topics and issues, especially AIDS. It is the most common source of information for youths because of its entertainment value as well as its accessibility and low costs. HIV/AIDS information from radio and television in form of advertisements, news, and live show constitutes the major ways through which adolescents gain HIV information. Many research findings are continually been published in this direction, with the hope that a successful prevention programs will checkmate the populace against indiscriminate sexual behavior, adopt safe sex practices, and internalize AIDS risk-reduction behaviors. In order to achieve this goal, government of various nations and other stakeholders which included international bodies and donors agencies have supported and implement a number of enlightenment programs worldwide. In Nigeria, there are weekly radio programs designed to disseminate family planning, HIV/AIDS, and other reproductive health information sponsored by the VISION Project (Keating et al., 2006). Society for Family Health had also sponsored different radio drama aimed at increasing awareness of HIV/AIDS. Included in these series are one thing at a time, Garin Muna Fata (Town of Hope), Odenjiji, and Abule Oloke Merin. There were other television, radio, printed materials, and organized outreach programs (lecture, seminar, workshop, peer-led education) geared toward educating the populace about the menace of HIV/AIDS and attendant consequences associated with unprotected sex. The ultimate goal is to achieve drastic reduction in the prevalence rate of three to six percent of adult population.

A number of studies have documented a substantial positive impact of HIV/AIDS prevention programs. (Mulusa, 1999; Harvey et al., 2000; Goodrich, 1999; Trangsrug, 1998; Nair, 1998; Sankararayan et al., 1996; Bhende, 1995; Chuamanochan, 1997; Renne, 1998; Ndeki et al., 1994; and Lewicky and Wheeler, 1996). Although a substantial number of the reviewed studies converge on the positive impact of education/enlightenment campaigns on prevention programmes, there are few divergent views on the most effective method. While Perry, Killen, Telch, Slinkard, and Damaher (1980) observed that in programs attempting to bring about behavior change among adolescents, peer-led health education has been demonstrated to be an effective method of programme delivery. Temin, Okonofua, Omorodion, Renne, Coplan, Heggen Hougen, and Kaufman (1999); Oyediran, Ishola, and Adedimeji (1998) studies considered media campaigns as the best way to educate young people about the disease and condom use.

Adolescents, by virtue of a number of behavioral and social characteristics, are more at risk in contracting HIV infection than any other development groups. Of many factors which predispose them to high risk include the early onset of sexual activity during the teen years (Feyisesan and Pabley, 1989; Oladepo and Brieger, 2000; Osowole and Oladepo, 2000); the probability of multiple partnerships (Ojwang and Naggwa, 1991; Fawole et al., 1991; and Okpani and Okpani, 2000); general nonuse or inconsistent use of condoms (More and Rosenthal, 1991; Fawole et al., 1999); and the reported tendency of adolescents to perceive themselves to both physically and psychologically invulnerable which in turn is related to the conduct of a variety of risk behaviours (More and Rosenthal, 1991; Swart-Kruger and Richer, 1997). Varnier et al., (1998) have noted that in areas of high HIV seroprevalence, infection will most likely occur in adolescence with early sexual exposure and therefore suggests that programs must educate adolescents about the risk involved with specific behavior and how to reduce those risks.

The objective of this study is to assess the influence of HIV/AIDS enlightenment campaigns on adolescents' sexual behaviour practices and their knowledge, attitudes, and beliefs about HIV/AIDS. Adolescents have become a focal point on discussions of sexuality and reproductive health matters because they belong to a most active segment of the population and because of practical concerns on resolving problems such as unintended pregnancy and sexually transmitted diseases (STDs), including HIV/AIDS (Alubo, 2001). Three hypotheses were formulated. The first hypothesis stated that HIV/AIDS enlightenment campaign programs disseminated through broadcast media will have more significant positive influence on adolescents' sexual behaviors than those disseminated through print media and organized activities. Hypothesis 2 stated that HIV/AIDS enlightenment campaign programs disseminated through broadcast media will have more significant influence on adolescents' knowledge, attitudes, and beliefs (KAB) about HIV/AIDS than those disseminated through print media and organized activities. The third hypothesis states that there will be a significant relationship between adolescents' exposure to enlightenment campaigns and their sexual behavior so that those highly exposed will have lower sexual risk behaviors than those with lower exposure.

METHODS

SAMPLE

The sample consisted of 1902 (917 males and 985 females) adolescents from twenty secondary schools in five local governments areas of Ibadan metropolis, Nigeria. The participants' age ranged from twelve to twenty years with a mean of sixteen years and a standard deviation of 1.46. The students selected were stratified using their sex, age, class, and local government. This was done in order to have an unbiased and representative sample. Four secondary schools from each of the five local governments participated in the study. The sample comprised students from both single sex and mixed schools. Twelve mixed and eight single sex (four only boys and four girls only) schools participated in the study, and 825 students came from single sex schools, while the majority (1077) came from mixed schools.

MEASURES

Three measuring instruments were used in the study. They consisted of self-administered paper-and-pencil questionnaire whose items were purposely adapted for this study. The majority of the instrument items were generated through an extensive adaptation of Haour-Knipe. Fleury and Dubois-Arber (1999); LeBlanc (2000) and Adamchak, Bond, MacLaren, Magnani, Nelson, and Seltzer (2002) questionnaires used in previous studies of a similar nature.

The questionnaire, which comprised mostly structured close-ended items, was divided into four sections. The first section sought for sociodemographic information from each respondent. The second section addressed the sources of HIV/AIDS awareness campaigns exposed to and perceived influence of these programs on adolescents. Section 3 of the questionnaire focused on adolescents' sexual behavior practices, which included current sexual activities, number of sexual partners, condom use, frequency, and rate of sexual intercourse and reasons for engaging in sexual activities. The last section of the questionnaire measured adolescents' knowledge attitudes and beliefs about HIV/AIDS.

HIV/AIDS ENLIGHTENMENT CAMPAIGNS SCALE

Items in this scale were directed to measure respondents' access to HIV/ AIDS enlightenment campaigns/awareness outlets. The scale focused on three areas: messages transmitted through broadcast media which include radio and television; information received from print media (books, magazine, posters, leaflets, bill boards, and so on); and enlightenment campaigns through organized activities (lectures, talks, symposium, debate, conference attendance, seminar and workshop participation, as well as information received from teachers, parents, role models, and religious bodies). There are twenty items for broadcast media, thirteen for print media, and thirteen items for organized activities. The scale has twenty-one major items; ten of which are with other sub-items ranging from two to eight. There are two different response categories for the items in this section. Forty-four of the items have Yes/No response category, while the remaining two items have response category that ranges from "daily to not at all."

Sample of the items include: "Have you at any time participated in any of these activities on HIV/AIDS?" (Debate, symposium, workshop, seminar, conference, rally) "Have you at any time had the opportunity of reading something on HIV/AIDS from any of these materials?" (Leaflets, handbills, poster, pamphlet, magazine, books, newspapers). "Have you at any time listened to radio or watch television program showing any of these on HIV/AIDS? (Life show, drama, jingles, advertisement, news).

All response categories with Yes/No were coded and scored as Yes=2; No= 1. The other two items were coded and scored: Daily-5; Almost Daily 4; 2-3 times per week-3; Weekly-2; Occasionally-1; and Not at All-0. The score obtainable in this section ranges between 46-100. The score were grouped into two halves using fiftieth percentile as the cut-off mark. Based on this, respondent were classified into two groups. Those with scores above fiftieth percentile value were categorized as "highly informed" group, while those with scores below the fiftieth percentile were labelled "informed group." The composite scores obtained by respondents in this section represent their measures on enlightenment campaign and were used in conjunction with their group category in the statistical analyses.

ADOLESCENTS' SEXUAL BEHAVIOR SCALE

The scale addressed adolescents' sexual activities especially in the last twelve months. It assessed their current number of sexual partners; age of first sexual experience; incidence and prevalence of sexual intercourse in the last one to three months before the survey; incidence of sexually transmitted diseases; reasons for engaging in sexual intercourse; and their experiences in a number of penetrative and nonpenetrative vaginal intercourses. It also examined the degree of sexual pressure and coercion on adolescents as well as their opinion and attitudes toward exchange of money and gift items for sex. The use of condom before and during the last sexual intercourse was also explored.

Sample of the items included: "Have you ever been forced against your will to have sexual intercourse?" "How old were you when you first had sexual intercourse?" "During the past thirty days, how often have you had sexual intercourse?" "Do you currently have a boy/girlfriend?" and "Have you done any of these activities in the last six months (holding hands, kissing, hugging, genital fondling, and sexual intercourse)?"

There are twenty-five major items in this section. Two of the items have another five items under it. Twenty-one of these items have Yes/No as their response category, while the remaining items have diverse response categories. Example include: Agree/Disagree, Regularly/Never; Unhappy/Happy; More frequently/Not at All. Each item was scored based on the response category it belongs to. "Yes/No" and "Agree/Disagree" were coded and scored as "2" or "1," respectively. Other response categories were coded and scored as applicable to their peculiar characteristics. These range between 0 to 5 depending on the type of item. Twenty of these items were used in calculating the composite scores for the respondents. The remaining five was excluded because of the nature of the items. For example, some of the items focused on the age of sexual partners, duration of friendship before sexual intercourse, and number of partners the respondent had intercourse with in the last twelve months. The sum of the items was obtained for each respondent, which vary between 20-48. The summated scores were treated as measures on interval scale and represent the score for each respondent on sexual behavior. These scores were used in all the statistical analyses in which the variable was needed for inferential analyses.

KNOWLEDGE, ATTITUDES, AND BELIEFS (KAB) SCALE

Knowledge, attitudes, and beliefs (KAB) scale has twenty-four items. Twelve of these items measured knowledge about HIV/AIDS: modes of transmission, incubatory period, and prevention. Six items assessed adolescents' beliefs about the disease in terms of existence, curability, and susceptibility. The last six items were included to measure respondents' attitudes toward the disease and related factors. Items on attitudes included attitudes toward sex as a result of the disease, right of a woman to insist on condom use, fear and anxiety associated with, and beliefs about HIV/AIDS.

Sample of items on the scale are: "A person can get AIDS through circumcision," "Do you believe that AIDS exists?" "AIDS is curable in some cases," "What I have heard has helped me to be afraid of HIV/AIDS," and "Information and campaigns about HIV/AIDS has helped me to say no to sex and reduce number of sexual partners." There are two major response categories in this section: "Agree/Disagree" and "Yes/No." Each respondent is left with the option of picking either of the two alternatives for each item.

In coding for data entry, "Agree" and "Yes" were coded and scored as a "2," while "Disagree" and "No" were coded and scored "1." These scored were added and translated to a composite score, which ranges from 24-48 for the respondents. All positive and favorable items retain their codes as scores on various items, while all negative and unfavorable items were recoded into same variable as Agree/Yes=1 and Disagree/No=2 during the data-editing stage of the analysis. The composite scores obtained for the respondents were grouped into two categories based on percentiles, and respondents were classified into high and low category based on their scores, which was either above the fiftieth percentile (high) or below the fiftieth percentile (low). Apart from each respondent's score, which was measured on interval scale, two groups (high/low) emerged and were measured on nominal scale. These two classifications and composite scores were used in subsequent statistical analyses. The composite scores derived from this section measures respondents' knowledge, attitudes, and beliefs about HIV/AIDS, and the two groups represent the levels.

VALIDITY AND RELIABILITY OF THE RESEARCH INSTRUMENTS

Beside the establishment of face and content validity of the instruments, construct validity of the instruments were also examined. Knowledge, Attitudes, and Beliefs (K AB) Scale and Adolescents Sexual Behaviours Scale were paired against relevant sections of a modified version WHO (KABP) questionnaire. Sections on knowledge and sexual practices were administered along the original questionnaire during the pilot testing. This is with the view of obtaining a correlation coefficient between the constructed version and similar one. This procedure is consistent with Anastasi and Urbania (1997) and Breakwell, Hammond, and Fife-Schaw (2000) positions on construct validity in which correlation between a new test and similar earlier test are cited as evidence that the new test measures approximately the same general area of behavior. A coefficient of 0.732 was obtained for Knowledge, Attitudes, and Beliefs Scale, while Adolescents' Sexual Behaviour Scale yielded 0.845.

The third instrument was paired with some items on channels of communication listed in the National Health Interview Survey (NHIS) questionnaire used in LeBlanc (2000) study. The 1987 version of NHIS contained a supplemental set of questions relating to HIV/AIDS and sources of HIV-related information. Results of the pilot study revealed a positive correlation between HIV/AIDS Enlightenment Campaign Scale and relevant section of NHIS questionnaire. The coefficient of correlation is given as 0.761.

Beyond these coefficients obtained for these instruments, various Cronbach's alpha coefficients obtained during the measure of internal consistency of test items can also be taken as a kind of construct validity (Breakwell et al., 2000)

> The measure of stability and internal consistency methods were used to ascertain the reliability of the instruments.

In establishing the stability of the scales, a pilot study was conducted among one hundred twenty adolescents considered a prototype of the sample. The test items were administered twice, with a two-week interval using a test-retest method. Scores obtained by each respondent on two occasions were correlated using Pearson (r) product moment correlation analysis to obtain the reliability coefficient for the test-retest. A coefficient of r=0.972 was obtained for enlightenment campaign scale, r=0.840 for Knowledge, Attitudes, and Beliefs (KAB) Scale, while Sexual Behaviors scale yielded r=0.953. All the three coefficient of correlation were significant at P<0.01 level.

Three methods were also employed to determine the internal consistency of the instruments. Each of the three scales was subjected to Cronbach alpha test, split half, and parallel form analysis. Knowledge, Attitudes, and Beliefs (KAB) Scale yielded Cronbach alpha coefficient of 0.6642; 0.7909 for split half, and estimated reliability of 0.7642 was obtained for parallel method with 0.0567 estimated common inter-item correlation. A Cronbach alpha coefficient of 0.8318 was recorded for enlightenment campaigns scale. When subjected to split half, it yielded a correlation coefficient of 0.5791 between forms, 0.7142 for part one, and 0.7783 for part two. The parallel method yielded 0.8318 as estimated reliability of the scale and 0.0786 as estimated common inter-items correlation. Sexual behaviors scale obtained a Cronbach alpha coefficient of 0.7731 and 0.5849 between forms on split half method with 0.8091 for part one and 0.7620 for part two of the scale. The parallel method yielded an estimated reliability of 0.7731 and estimated common inter-item correlation of 0.1158.

PROCEDURES

Data were collected from all the selected school students using the prepared paper-and-pencil self-report questionnaire. Principals and school counselors of the selected twenty schools in Ibadan metropolis were contacted through personal letters from the researcher before the administration of the questionnaire for their consent and cooperation.

Fifty students from the psychology and philosophy departments at Obafemi Awolowo University served as research assistants for the study. Ten of these students were used as coordinators for the five local government areas, monitoring the activities of other students sent to the selected schools. Two students were sent to each of the selected twenty schools with the pack of questionnaire meant for the selected students. The data collection was done in each school with the assistance of school counselor in that school and other designated teacher/officer by the principal/vice principal. For ease of administration, the students drawn from each of the classes were pooled together in a quiet area within the school premises. Instructions on how to complete the questionnaire, which had been printed on the questionnaire, were read to the group of selected adolescents by the research assistants. The completed questionnaires were collected at the end of a specified period, which ranged between twenty20 and thirty minutes.

RESULTS

The first hypothesis stated that HIV/AIDS enlightenment campaign programs disseminated through broadcast media will have a more significant positive influence on adolescents' sexual behaviors than those disseminated through print media and organized activities. Multiple regression analysis was conducted to test the hypothesis. Adolescents' scores on three types of exposure to enlightenment campaigns and their sexual behaviours were used in the analysis.

Table 1
Multiple Regression Analysis on the Influence of HIV/AIDS
Enlightenment Campaign on Adolescents Sexual Behaviors

VARIABLES (S) ENTERED ON STEPWISE METHOD.

1. BRODMED—Broadcast media
2. PRITMED—Print media.
3. PRGACTV—Organized activities.
   MULTIPLE R—0.227
   R-SQUARE—0.052
   ADJUSTED R—0.05
   STANDARD ERROR—4.126

Variables in the Equation

VARIABLE	B	SE B	Beta	T	Sig. T
BRODMED	0.357	0.041	0.217	8.769	0.0001
PRINTMED	-0.262	0.053	-0.120	-4.980	0.0001
ORGACTV	0.110	0.048	0.056	2.310	0.021
CONSTANT	14.726	1.150	-	12.810	0.0001

Results in Table 1 indicates that there is significant low relationship between the three types of exposure to enlightenment campaigns and sexual behaviors (Multiple R=0.227). The regression equation with all the three predictors is significantly related to the sexual behaviors of adolescents R^2=0.052, adjusted R^2=0.05, F (3,1897)=34.483, P<0.0001. R-square which shows the joint contribution of the independent variables (broadcast media, print media, and organized activities) to the dependent variable (sexual behavior) showed that these independent variables jointly contribute 5 percent (5.2) of the variance in sexual behavior.

When examined for the best overall predictor, broadcast media was found to contribute most to the variance observed in sexual behavior with β=0.217, t=8.769, P<0.0001; compared with print media, β=0.120, t=-4.980, P<0.001; and organized activities, β-0.056, t=2.310, P<0.021. Further observation revealed that of the five percent variance obtained, broadcast media accounted for 3.8 percent (R=0.96,

R^2=-.038, F (1,1899)=75.727, P<0.0001), while broadcast media and print media jointly contributed 4.8 percent of the variance (R=0.221, R^2=0.049, F(2,1898)=48.945, P<0.0001. This means that HIV/AIDS enlightenment campaigns disseminated through broadcast media has more significant positive influence on adolescents' sexual behaviors than those disseminated through print media and organized activities. The hypothesis is, therefore, accepted and retained.

Hypothesis 2 stated that HIV/AIDS enlightenment campaign programs disseminated through broadcast media will have more significant influence on adolescents' knowledge, attitudes, and beliefs (KAB) about HIV/AIDS than those disseminated through print media and organized activities. The result of multiple regression analysis conducted to evaluate how broadcast media predicted adolescents' knowledge, attitudes, and beliefs (KAB) about HIV/AIDS over the print media and organized activities is presented in Table 2.

Table 2

Multiple Regression Analysis on the Influence of Three Methods of HIV/AIDS enlightenment campaign on Adolescents' Knowledge, Attitudes and Beliefs about HIV/AIDS.

Variables (s) entered on stepwise method.
1. BRODMED—Broadcast media
2. PRITMED—Print media.
3. ORGANCTV—Organized activities.
    Multiple R—0.232
    R-square—0.054
    Adjusted R-square—0.053
    Standard Error—2.272

Variables in the Equation

Variable	B	SE.B	Beta	T	Sig. T
PRITMED	0.295	0.028	0.246	10.358	0.0001
BRODMED	-9.108E-02	0.022	-0.100	-4.233	0.0001
CONSTANT	24.121	0.614	-	39.281	0.0001

Excluded, P< 0.05

The results indicates a significant linear combination of print media and broadcast media on adolescents' knowledge, attitudes, and beliefs (KAB) about HIVAIDS, F (2,1898)=53.963, P<0.0001. Organized activities had no significant influence on knowledge, attitudes, and beliefs about HIV/ AIDS, (R=0.007, P≥0.387), t=-1.381, P>0.168; hence, it was excluded from the stepwise regression analysis (p>0.05). The sample multiple correlation coefficient was 0.232, indicating that approximately 5.4 percent of the variance of adolescents' knowledge, attitudes, and beliefs about HIV/AIDS can be accounted for by the linear combination of broadcast and print media.

There is a significant relationship between print media and knowledge, attitudes, and beliefs of participants(R=0.212, P<0.0001), as well as between broadcast media and knowledge, attitudes, and beliefs scores (R=-0.181, P<0.001). On examination for the best overall predictor, print media was found to contribute more to the variance observed in knowledge, attitudes, and beliefs (KAB) about HIV/AIDS, β=0.246, t=10.358, P<0.0001 against broad cast media, β=-0.100, t=-4.233, P<0.0001. It was further observed that out of the 5.3 percent variance in adolescents' knowledge, attitudes, and beliefs (KAB) about HIV/AIDS, print media accounted for 4.5 percent (R=0.212, R^2= 0.45, F (1,1899)=89.210, P<0.0001. Based on the results, HIV/AIDS enlightenment campaigns disseminated through broadcast media did not have a more significant influence on adolescents' knowledge, attitudes, and beliefs about HIV/AIDS than those disseminated through print media and organized activities. On the contrary, it was print media that exerted a more significant influence on adolescents' knowledge, attitudes, and beliefs about HIV/AIDS more than broadcast media, while organized activities had no significant influence at all.

Recall that hypothesis 3 stated that there will be a significant relationship between exposure to HIV/AIDS enlightenment campaign programs and sexual behaviors of adolescents so that those in the highly exposed group would have lower sexual risks behaviors than those in the lower exposed group. Adolescents' composite scores on exposure to campaigns enlightenment were grouped into two (informed and highly informed) using fiftieth percentile and subjected to two-way ANOVA with some other independent variables. The result of the analysis is presented in Table 3.

Table 3

Influence of Enlightenment Campaigns and Knowledge,
Attitudes and Beliefs on Adolescents' Sexual Behaviors

	Dependent Variable: (Sexual Behavior)				
Source	Type III Sum of Squares	df	MeanSquare	F	Sig.
Corrected Model	766.602	5	153.320	9.312	.000
Intercept	709047.914	1	709047.914	43065.422	.000
Enlightenment	206.016	1	206.016	12.513	.000
Knowledge, Attitudes, and Beliefs (KAB)	500.807	2	250.403	15.209	.000
Enlightenment* KAB	2.239	2	1.120	.068	.934
Error	31216.572	1896	16.464		
Total	859189.881	1902			
Corrected Total	31983.174	1901			

As seen in table three, the F-value for the exposure to enlightenment campaign main effect, $F(1,196)=12.513$; $p<0.001$, exceeds the tabled critical value $F=3.84$ at $P\leq 0.05$ with df=1 and $df_2=\propto$. Therefore, hypothesis 3 is confirmed that HIV/AIDS enlightenment campaigns had significant influence on adolescents' sexual behaviors. A follow-up pair-wise comparison test between highly informed group and informed group revealed a mean difference of 0.665 with standard error of 0.199, which is significant at 0.001. Also, there was a significant main effect of knowledge, attitudes, and beliefs on adolescents' sexual behavior, $F(2,1896)=15.209$; $p<0.001$, but no interaction effect exist between enlightenment campaigns and knowledge, attitudes, and beliefs on adolescents' sexual behavior, $F(2,1896)=0.068$;$p=.934$.

DISCUSSION

The findings from this study revealed that all the major independent variables—exposure to enlightenment campaigns, knowledge, attitudes, and beliefs about HIV/AIDS—influenced adolescents' sexual behaviors.

Hypothesis 1 compares the influence of broadcast media with other HIV/AIDS enlightenment campaigns on adolescents' sexual behaviors. The results obtained showed that broadcast media (television and radio) had a greater influence on sexual behaviors than print media and organized activities. The finding that broadcast media, specifically radio, could positively impact behavior change is consistent with Farr et al. (2005) and Benefo (2004) who found that radio programming was more effective in facilitating behavioral change than any other media. It is also evident from research that a multipronged approach to media messaging is more successful than using a single method (Selikow et al., 2006); however, this research clearly suggests that radio and television were more effective in influencing sexual behaviors than print media and other organized activities. This might be due to the fact that broadcast media (particularly radio) were the most popular means for receiving information (Shisana et al., 2005; Benefo, 2004; Keating, Meekers, and Adewuyi, 2006) followed by television and the printed media. Lewicky and Wheeler (1996) also found that radio constituted the major source of information on HIV/AIDS, where about 94 percent of youth surveyed listened to radio at least one day per week. The finding of Fawole et al. (1999) is also consistent with what we obtained in this study. They found that intensive radio outreach and sensitization seminars as most effective in changing attitudes on sexuality and reproductive health. Betrand et al. (2006) conducted a review of twenty-four studies of the effectiveness of mass media interventions and found consistent media effects on risks reduction behaviors.

Despite our finding, some researches indicate no significant relationship between type of media exposure and behavior. Keating, Meekers, and Adewuyi (2006) found no significant difference between media and behavior. Benefo (2004) also found that program exposure of any type had no significant impact on reported condom use at last sexual intercourse.

The results of hypothesis 2 shows that print media exerted significantly more influence on adolescents' knowledge, attitudes, and beliefs about HIV/AIDS than did broadcast media (radio and television), while organized activities had no effect on HIV knowledge, attitudes, and beliefs. This was surprising to us since we hypothesized that television and radio would have a significantly greater effect on HIV/AIDS knowledge, attitudes, and beliefs than print media. One basic assumption about this discovery is that information received from print media or reading materials such as books, magazines, newspapers, posters, and billboards had a more significant influence on people's knowledge because it is more than mere exposure, such as in the case with broadcast media. The attention needed for print media are more concentrated and for a longer period than television-featured advertisements, jingles, and radio programs. These television programs may only last for a few seconds or minutes, as appose to print media which an individual can keep with them for an extended period of time. Beneto's findings are inconsistent with our findings in that he discovered that radio media was more important than other mass media in enhancing knowledge of HIV/AIDS prevention. There is the tendency of going back to the materials consulted or made available in the form of leaflets, newsletter, and pamphlets which provide opportunity for reappraisal and assessment of the information provided. There is the possibility that information from print media has a way of impinging on the individual's cognitive information processing based on rational objective assessments than those flickered through the television in a moment. Individuals may easily forget what they see or hear in seconds but internalize more of what they take time to read, digest, and assimilate. (Selikow et al., 2006)

Prior research has observed that television programs and advertisement (both free and paid for media coverage) have been the main sources of AIDS information for all age groups (Wallack, 1981; Flay, 1987; and Redman et al., 1990). As noted in the literature review, leaflets and the print media are secondary sources of information, while family and friends are very much a subsidiary source.

On the third hypothesis, it was discovered that a significant relationship exists between adolescents' exposure to enlightenment campaigns and sexual behavior but not in the expected direction. It was expected that adolescents that were more exposed to all forms of HIV/AIDS enlightenment campaigns would be cautious and engage in less sexual risk activities than those exposed to less enlightenment campaigns; however, the result obtained revealed the opposite. The highly exposed adolescents took more sexual risk than the exposed group. Engle et al. (1993) and Kirby (1989) support our finding on exposure to enlightenment campaign, which revealed that adolescents' knowledge about sex does not always match their behavior. These studies observed that sexuality education programs increase knowledge about sexuality, but there is little evidence that they change attitudes or behaviors. The finding is also consistent with Christopher and Rossa (1991) findings on evaluation study of an abstinence education programs (the "success express" program) targeted at a group of low-income minority group youths in Arizona. The study found no desired change in attitudes or behavior; rather, more young men in the intervention group than in the control group claimed to have initiated intercourse by the end of the program.

Some research has suggested that individuals are more likely to change as a result of the discussion of campaigns rather than as a direct result of the discussion of campaigns rather than as a direct result of messaging itself (Hornik, 2002; Noar, 2006). This result is also in line with Wilson and Levelle (1990) which confirmed that behavior modification is best achieved by small group, face-to-face, participative, and community-based approaches rather than large scale campaigns. Chubb and Vandijk (2001) reported adoption of old traditions of storytelling and youth literature as a new methods of AIDS education among South African youths based on the limited success recorded from information campaigns. This is consistent with Agha and Van Rossem (2002) who observed that a substantial body of communication literature based on experience in developed countries has shown that mass media campaigns are not sufficient in themselves to produce change in behaviors.

Despite our findings, some studies have found adolescent behavioral change to be possible through the use of enlightenment/awareness campaigns. Rotheram-Borus et al. (1991) gave educational session directed at general knowledge and coping skills to sixty-seven runaways at a nonintervention shelter and found after the sessions young people reported more consistent condom use and less high-risk sexual behaviors.

Barth et al. (1992) also reported on sex education program delivered to high school students which aimed at increasing knowledge and student-parent communication. The results showed that the experimental curriculum increased students' knowledge and improved communication with parents on sexual health matters. Selikow et al., 2006 suggests a similar idea that mass media campaigns alone cannot facilitate behavior change among adolescents but that a multipronged approach to media, theory-led initiatives of behavior change, dealing with multiple sources of conflicting information, and challenging traditional ideas of masculinity and femininity all play a role in ensuring the effectiveness of HIV/AIDS enlightenment campaigns.

REFERENCES

Abramson, P.R.; Sekler, J.C.; Berk, R.; Cloud, M.Y. (1989) "An Evaluation of an Undergraduate Course on AIDS." *Evaluation Review.* 1989, 13: 516-32

Agha, S. and Van Rossem, R. (2002). "Impact of Mass Media Campaigns on Intentions to Use the Female Condom in Tanzania." *International Family Planning Perspectives*, Vol. 28(3), Sept., 151-157.

Ajuwon, A.J.; Olley, B.O.; Akin-Jimoh, I.; and Akintola, A. (2001) "Experience of Sexual Coercion among Adolescents in Ibadan, Nigeria." African Journal of Reproductive Health, 5(3) 120-130.

Alubo, O. (2001) "Adolescent Reproductive Health Practices in Nigeria." *African Journal of Reproductive Health*; 5(3); 109-119.

Araoye, M.O. and Fakeye, O.O. (1998) "Sexuality and Contraception among Nigerian Adolescents and Youth." *African Journal of Reproductive Health,* 2 (2); 142-150.

Barth, R.P., Fetro, J.V.; Leland, N.; and Volkan, K. (1992) "Preventing Adolescent Pregnancy with Social and Cognitive Skills." Journal of Adolescent Research, 7:208-32.

Benefo, K. D. (2004). "The Mass Media and HIV Prevention in Ghana." Journal of Health and Population in Developing Countries, 1-18.

Bertrand, J.T., K. O'Reilly, J., Denison, R., Anhang, and M. Sweat. 2006. "Systematic Review of the Effectiveness of Mass Communication Programs to Change HIV/AIDS-Related Behaviors in Developing Countries." *Health Education Research,* 21:567-597.

Bhende, A.A (1995) "Evolving a Model for AIDS Prevention Education among Underprivileged Adolescent Girls in Urban India." *Interventional center for Research on Women (IC.RW) Women* and AIDS Research Program Research Report Series. 1-5.

Cahs, K., Sanguan Sermri, J., Busayawong, W., and Chuamanochan, P. (1997) *AIDS Prevention through Peer Education for Northern.*

Christopher, F.S., Roosa, M.W. (1990). "An Evaluation of an Adolescent Pregnancy Prevention Program: Is Just say No enough?" *Family Relations.* 39:68-72.

Chubb, K. and Van Dijk, L. (2001) Youth Literature and Storytelling: A Different Approach to AIDS Education in South Africa. *Sexual Health Exchange.*

Diclemente, R.J., Boyer, C.B., and Morales, E.S. (1988) "Minorities and AIDS: Knowledge, Attitudes, and Misconceptions among Black and Latino Adolescents." *American Journal of Public Health* 78 (1):55-57.

Djohan E (2001) "Evaluation of the Youth Center Programme of Eight IPPA Chapters, West Sumatera. Exclusive summary. Unpublished paper. *Centre for Population and Manpower Studies,* Indonesian Institute of Sciences Indonesia, 1-9

Engel, J.W., Saracino, M., and Bergen, M.B. (1993) Sexuality Education. In Arcus, M.E., Schvaneveldt, J.D., and Moss, J.J. (eds) *Handbook of Family Life Education: The Practice of Family Life Education* (Vol. 2) Newbury Park, C.A., Sage.

Farr, A.C., Witte, K., Jarto, K., and Menard, T. (2005). "The Effectiveness of Media Use in Health Education: Evaluation of an HIV/AIDS Television Campaign in Ethiopia. *Journal of Health Communication, 10,* 225-235.

Fawole, O.I., Azuzu, M.C., and Oduntan, S.O. (1999). "Survey of Knowledge, Attitudes, and Sexual Practices Relating to HIV Infection/AIDS among Nigerian Secondary School Students." *African Journal of Reproductive Health.* 392: 15-24.

Feyisetan, B. and Pebley, A. R. (1989) "Premarital Sexuality in Urban Nigeria." *Studies in Family Planning,* 20 (6); 343-54.

Flay, B. R. (1987). "Mass Media and Smoking Cessation: A Critical Review." *American Journal of Public Health, 77,* 153-160

Harvey, B., Stuart, J., and Swan, T. (2000) "Evaluation of a Drama-In-Education Programme to Increase AIDS Awareness in South Africa High Schools." A randomized community intervention trail. *International Journal of STDs and AIDS,* 11(2) 105-11.

Hornik, R. C. (2002). Preface. Public Health Communication: Evidence for Behavior Change. R. C. Hornik. Mahwah, N. J., Lawrence Erlbaum Associates

Izugbara, C.O (2001) "Tasting the Forbidden Fruit: The Social Context of Debut Sexual Encounters among Young Persons in a Rural Nigerian Community." *African Journal of Reproductive Health*; 5 (2): 22-29.

Keating, J., Meekers, D., Adewuyi, A. "Assessing Effects of a Media Campaign on HIV/AIDS Awareness and Prevention in Nigeria: Results from the VISION Project." BMC Public Health 2006; 6:123.

Kirby, D (1989) "Research on Effectiveness of Sex Education Programmes." *Theory into Practice*, 28(3); 165-171.

LeBlanc, A.J. (2000): "Examining HIV-Related Knowledge among Adults in the U.S." In Lemelle, A. J. et al. (Ed) *Readings in the Sociology of AIDS*. New Jersey, Prentice Hall Inc.

Lema, V.M. and Mulandi, T.N. (1992) Knowledge, Attitudes, and Practices Related to AIDS and HIV Infection among Adolescents in Kenya." Unpublished paper. *Centre for the Study of Adolescence*. Nairobi, Kenya. Vii 1-84

Lewicky, N and Wheeler, M. (1996) "HIV/AIDS and Adolescents: Key Funding from the Youth HIV/AIDS Baseline Survey in Seven Districts of Uganda. Unpublished paper. Delivery of Improved Services for Health Project.

McAlister, A., Perry, C., Killer, J., Sinkard, L.A., and MacCoby, N. (1980). "Pilot Study of Smoking Alcohol and Drug Abuse Prevention." *American Journal of Public Health*, 70; 719-721.

Moore, S. and Rosenthal, D. (1991). "Condoms and Coctus: Adolescents' Attitudes to AIDS and Safe Sex." *Journal of Adolescence*, 14; 211-227.

Mulusa, M. (1999). "Uganda: The Sexually Transmitted Infections Project." *Findings, Knowledge, and Learning Center,* Africa Region, World Bank.

Nair, S. (1998) "Catch 'Em Young: A Best Practice Case Study on School Based AIDS Preventive Education Programmes in Maharashtral, India" 24.

Noar, S. M. (2006). "A 10-Year Retrospective of Research in Health Mass Media Campaigns: Where Do We Go from Here?" *Journal of Health Communication*, 11(1), 21-42.

Ndeki, S.S., Klepp, K.I., Seha, A.M., and Leshabari, M.T. (1994) "Exposure to HIV/AIDS Information: AIDS Knowledge, Perceived Risk, and Attitudes toward People with AIDS among Primary School Children in Northern Tanzania." AIDS CARE, 6(2); 183-91.

Oakelly, A., Fullerton, D., Holland, J., Arnold, S., France-Dawson, M., Kelly, P., and McGrellis, S. (1995). "Sexual Health Education Interventions for Young People: A Methodological Review." *British Medical Journal*, 310: 158-162.

Ojwang, S.B.O. and Maggwa, A.B.N. (1991). "Adolescent Sexuality in Kenya." *East African Medical Journal,* 68; 74-80.

Okpani, A.O.U. and Okpani, J.U. (2000) "Sexual Activity and Contraceptive Use among Female Adolescents: A Report from Port Harcourt, Nigeria. *African Journal of Reproductive Health,* 4 (1): 40-47.

Oladepo, O. and Brieger, W. (2000). "Sexual Attitudes and Behavior of Male Secondary School Students in Rural and Urban Areas." *African Journal of Reproductive Health*, 4(2), 21-34.

Osowele, O. S. and Oladepo, O. (2000) "Effect of Peer Education on Deaf Secondary School Students' HIV/AIDS Knowledge, Attitudes, and Sexual Behavior." *African Journal of Reproductive Health,* 4 (2); 93-103

Oyediran, K.A., Ishola, G., Adedimeji, A. (1998) "Impact of Peer education on the Reproductive Health of In-And-Out-Of-School youth in Ibadan." Evaluation findings; 1995-1997. Association for Reproductive and Family Health 1998; ARFH Monograph series No. 4.

Pattulo, A.L., Malonza, M., Kimani, G.G., Muthee, A., Otieno, P.A., Odihiambo, K., Moses, S., and Plummer, F.A. (1994) "Survey of Knowledge, Behaviour, and Attitudes Relating to HIV Infection and AIDS among Kenyan Secondary School Students. *AidsCare*; 6 (2); 173-181.

Perry, C., Killen, J., Telch, M., Slinkard. L.A., and Danaher, B. (1980) "Modifying Smoking Behavior of Teenagers: A School-Based Intervention." *American Journal of Public Health,* 70:722-725

Redman, S., Spencer, E.A., and Sanson-Fisher, R.W. (1990), "The Role of Mass Media in Changing Health-Related Behavior: A Critical Appraisal of Two Models." *Health Education Research Theory and Practice*, 5 (1), 85-94.

Richter, D.L., Strack, R.W., Vincent, M.L., Barnes, B., and Rao, R. (1997) Sexual and AIDS-Related Knowledge, Attitudes, and Behaviors of Adolescents in Sierra Leone, West Africa." *International Quarterly of Community Health Education* 16(4), 371-381.

Rotheram-Borus, M.J., Koopman, C., Haignere, C., Davies, M. (1991) "Reducing HIV Sexual Risk Behaviors among Runaway Adolescents." *Journal of American Medical Association,* 266; 1237-41.

Sankaranaryan, S., Naik, E., Reddy, D.S., Gurumani, G., Gancsh, K., Gandewar, K., Singh,. K.P., and Vermund, S.H. (1996) "Impact of School-Based HIV and AIDS Education for Adolescents in Bombay, India." *Southeast Asian Journal of Tropical Medicine and Public Health.* Dec. 27(4). 692-5

Selikow, T., Flisher, A. J., Matthews, C., and Ketye, T. (2006). "Media Messaging: A Synthesis of Lessons from the Literature to Inform HIV Prevention amongst Young People." *Journal of Child and Adolescent Mental Health*, 18(2): 61-72

Shisana, O., Rehle, T., Simbayi, LC., Parker, W., Zuma, K., Bhana, K. (2005) "South African National HIV Prevalence, HIV Incidence, Behavior, and Communication Survey." Cape Town: Human Sciences Research Council Publishers.

Swart-Kruger, J. and Richter, L. (1994) "South African Adolescents and AIDS-Related Issues, with Specific on Black Street Children." In Le Roux, J (ed) *The Black Child in Crisis: A Socio-Educational Perspective* Pretoria, Van Schaik pp. 257-284.

Tabet, S. R., Voltural, A. M., Wallerstein, N., and Koster, F. T. (1992). Fear of AIDS: An Assessment of Knowledge and Attitudes and of Medical, Nursing, and Medical Technology Students." *Teaching and Learning in Medicine*, 4; 56-161.

Temin, M. J., Okonofua, F.E., Omorodion, F.O., Renne, E.P., Coplan, P., Heggenhougen, H.K., and Kaufman, J. (1999) "Perceptions of Sexual Behavior and Knowledge About Sexually Transmitted Diseases among

Adolescents in Benin City, Nigeria." *International Family Planning Perspectives.* 1999, 25 (4); 186-90.—

Trangsrug, R. (1998) "Adolescent Reproductive Health in East and Southern Africa: Building Experience." Four case studies. *Regional Adolescent Reproductive Health Network* 58, 2.

Uwakwe, C. B. U. (1997). "Socioculture Factors That Predispose Women to HIV/AIDS in the Middle Belt of Nigeria." In Umeh, DC (Ed) "Confronting the AIDS Epidemic: Cross-Cultural Perspective on HIV/AIDS Education." Trenton, N. J. Africa World Press, Inc.

Wallack, L. M. (1981) "Mass Media Campaigns: The Odds against Finding Behavior Change. Health Education Quarterly. 8(3):209-60, 1981.

Wenger, N. S., Greenera, J. M., Hillborne, L. H., Kusseling, F., Mantogich, M., Shapiro, M. (1996) "Effect of HIV Antibody Testing and AIDS Education on Communication About HIV Risk and Sexual Behaviors: A Randomized Controlled Trial in College Students." *Annals of International Medicine,* 117; 905-911.

Wilson, D. and Lavelles, S. (1990) HIV/AIDS in Africa. *AidsCare,* 2(4); 371-375.

The Sociopolitics of Black Men and Criminality in the Media: Shaping Perception, Impression, and Affect Control

Dr. Sharon Zoe Spencer
Virginia State University Petersburg Virginia, USA

ABSTRACT

This work theoretically evaluates how the homogenous (stereotypical) presentations of African-American men, in mainstream media, serve as a dominant form of perception development and affect control that has social, political, and judicial implications that impede African-American men's access to opportunity, justice, and even the right to live freely. Utilizing the theoretical concepts of affect control (specifically the concept of impression formation) and ideological hegemony (Gramsci), this work will analyze how the controlled media presentation of the images of African-American men shape social perception, collective impression formation and ultimately guides social interaction, sociopolitical policy, and practice, and how "justice is (truly) served." It will address the cyclical implications of these presentations for not only the African-American race but also for other groups who rely (largely) on the media as their only source of identification for and information about the group and their culture.

INTRODUCTION

Society, through the media, has created an image where they have criminalized the culture and being of African-American men who resist conforming to European standards of normative presentation and acceptability. In such, African-American men, specifically urban youth, are identified and categorized by their very association to their race, class, and gender. Those who are privileged enough to belong to the middle and upper class often conform to traditional and mainstream cultural values and presentations that are often associated to the class in which they belong or risk being classified by members of their community as deviant. However, those who belong to either working class and/or urban inner city communities, where urban cultural values and presentations are the norm, are often labeled and criminalized by their very association to the race and gender constructs that are not undone or overridden by their class status. As Wilson (1996) argues in his work, *When Work Disappears,* "A reasonable hypothesis concerning behavior is that in stable neighborhoods, people who are economically marginal and are struggling to make ends meet are more strongly constrained to act in mainstream ways than are their counterparts in high jobless neighborhoods that feature problems of social organization and ghetto-related modes of adaptation" (p. 70). This "criminalization" is facilitated by media presentations that correlate a Black man's appearance, i.e., the way that he wears his hair (locks, braids, afros, or anything that is associated to his "Africanness"), his clothes, or even his dialect to criminality and/or forms of not secondary but primary deviance. In essence, the Black man, through the media, is criminalized by his very nature.

The image of the "Black man" that is promoted through news media, urban videos, and urban literature shapes the perception of those who would, otherwise, not have contact with the group and ultimately affects interaction, policy, law, and judicial outcome. In essence, not only are Black men "guilty until proven innocent," but they are guilty by association to their race, gender, class status, and the embrace of their urban culture. Consequently, those who are not familiar or who do not respect and/or understand Black or urban cultural identity as being separate from the criminality that occurs within urban/inner cities are often stimulated by media presentations to make a correlation between race and criminality—that does not allow Black men to be Black men without being criminalized. In his work, Hatcher (1995) asserts, "Racism, we are sometimes told, rests largely on ignorance. If we get to know people better, we will discover that they are quite different from what we have been led to think they are" (p. 24).

In order to truly understand the nature of the media and affect control, one cannot remove the current perceptions of Black male identity from its historic context. As a result of the institution of enslavement, Black men have been stereotyped and removed from their subjectivity and privilege as not only men but as human beings. Stereotypes that were originally constructed to justify the exploitation and control of Black men's freedom, productive, and reproductive labor precede the Transatlantic Slave Trade and include stereotypes such as biological and intellectual inferiority, savagery, hypersexuality, immorality, violence, aggression, and ultimately, criminality. Just as theorists, such as Cesare Lombroso (1876), promoted ideologies that historically linked the physical characteristics associated with the African race with biological and/or innate criminality, so now does the media promote the same? And although such theories have since been disproven, they have continued to permeate American society since African people reached the shores of these United States in the 1600s.

Consequently, unlike other races and ethnic groups whose oppression was predicated on the development of propagandist media campaigns that were developed to remove the group from its humanity and justify the oppression and even genocide of the group, without instigating resistance or rebellion, the correction of the fallacies for African-American people, specifically African-American men, has never been made. Therefore, the correlation between Black men and deviance has continued to serve as a "the reality" for American society. So consequently, when one moves to the present and begins to analyze how media presentations of African-American men continue to shape perceptions and affect, it becomes clearer that the historic stereotypes continue.

A THEORETICAL UNDERSTANDING OF THE MEDIA AS A SOCIOPOLITICAL TOOL

The presentation of Black men in cinema and other media is not a new topic. Leading the way in the study of the visual presentations are authors such as Donald Bogle (1973) who was one of the first to "tease out" the stereotypical constructs that emerged in mainstream cinema. However, one of the greatest limitations in the literature is its failure to ground the analysis and presentation of, not only Black men in the media, but also the media itself in a sociopolitical context. In such, it fails to root how and why the stereotypes are utilized. However, when the presentations of African-American men in the media are rooted in a sociopolitical context, it is found that both historic and contemporary presentations are just as much rooted in capitalism, specifically the way in which Black men's productive and reproductive labor are being exploited as they are in race—which oftentimes merely serves as a "justifier" for power relations and hierarchical stratification.

> "Blacks, the system dictated, needed to be kept in their place. When this occurred, whites received a variety of benefits. In a study conducted in another Southern town during the 1930s, John Dollard (1937) suggested that local middle class whites received three principal gains from their dominant position in the caste system. First, there was an economic benefit. Middle class whites were able to avoid menial, often physically demanding jobs. Second, Dollard discussed whites' sexual gain, meaning that because of their superior position in the caste structure, white men had unchallenged sexual access to both African-American and white women . . . Third . . . Southern Whites received prestige gain. Simply because people were white, they were able to demand forms of deference from Blacks that would enhance their self esteem" (Doobs 1993:22).

Many view the media as a harmless form of communication, information, and/or entertainment. However, the media is a "tool." And just like any tool, the tool only takes the form of those who control it. In all of its forms, "the media" represents a unilateral form mass communication that has the capacity to control how the public receives information and what information it receives (Hassan, 2001:33). Therefore, as a tool or even a weapon, as noted during the Nazi regime, specifically the manner in which the Reichminister of Propaganda, Joseph Goebbels manipulated the media in order to promote the genocidal agenda of the Nazi government during that time, the media has the capacity to be utilized as a means of shaping and controlling public perception; hence, conformity to ideologies and agendas that, as the Holocaust demonstrated, can be detrimental to a group if left unchecked. Be it the state or through private ownership, the media can, will, and has served the interest of those who control it. Contrary to the beliefs of many, the media, most predominantly the news media, that is often thought to be an objective presentation of information, is not absent of ownership and control. It is not only regulated by governmental agencies such as the Federal Communications Commission (FCC), but it is regulated and controlled by those who own it. Yes, even the news is owned.

The media, especially mainstream media, are largely owned by private individuals/media moguls or ruling class families who have an established legacy as economic stakeholders in the United States and abroad. Some of the more notable examples include: Katherine Meyer Graham, daughter and heir of Eugene Meyer, who owns *The Washington Post*, *Newsweek Magazine*, and several local and national television stations; Rupert Murdoch, who owns the *New York Post* and Fox News Network; and Ted Turner, who owns WTBS and TNT, and also owns CNN and Time Warner and was once owner of movie production house MGM/UA (MetroGoldwynMayer-United Artist). So just like any business, the information that is disseminated and the manner in which it is presented will be in, if not the interest of, under the control of its owner who will shape the personality, approach, and viewpoint of the information.

Historically, the media have been utilized to disseminate information, promote dominant ideologies, and ultimately control the perception of the masses, hence promote and maintain conformity to the status quo and minimize resistance to social, political, and economic agendas (Berberoglu 1998). From the historic media presentations of African and African-American people, to Reichminister Joseph Goebbels use of the media as a tool to promote the Nazi agenda during the Holocaust, to contemporary homogenous presentations of the Black man as the criminal man or the "thug," the media, in all of its forms, only takes the form and promotes the agenda of those who control it.

Theoretically, the works of Gramsci and Lenin (1918) place "the media" in a context that provides a foundation for understanding the media from a sociopolitical perspective. Spencer (2011) submits that *Lenin* argued that the state is an apparatus of the ruling class, represents *"the entire complex of practical and theoretical activities with which the ruling class not only justifies and maintains its dominance, but manages to win the active consent of those over whom it rules"* (Gramsci in Berberoglu, 1998:62). Subsequently, through utilizing what Gramsci terms the "super structural organs" of the state, which includes the media, the ruling class not only promotes the masses' conformity to, but even support for, the dominance of ruling-class ideologies and interests over their own ideologies, interests, and conditions.

Gramsci furthers:

> *"With the acceptance of its ideas and the legitimization of its rule, the capitalist class is able to exercise control and dominance of society through its ideological hegemony at the level of the superstructure with the aid and instrumentality of the state"* (in Berberoglu, 1998:62).

In essence, Lenin suggests that the media is just one of the tools that are utilized to promote and protect the interests of the ruling class. Gramsci furthers Lenin's argument by analyzing how the state is utilized to promote dominant ideologies that support the political and economic interests and agenda of the ruling class by promoting the masses' conformity to values, interests, and conditions that are often contrary to their own well-being. The elimination of coercion—that is achieved by/through promoting ideological hegemony—perpetuates and facilitates the "legitimization" of oppression that Gramsci argues results from the capitalist exploitation of labor.

A HISTORIC SUMMARY OF THE STEREOTYPICAL CONSTRUCTS OF BLACK MASCULINITY

While contemporary presentations of Black men in the media have become an issue in sociological, psychological, and criminological circles, neither is the manner in which Black men have been presented in the media new, nor is it without foundation. Works such as Bogle (1971), Wallace (1978), and Diawara (1993), just to name a few, have defined and analyzed the media constructions of African-American men in film. The constructs of the Buck, the Uncle Tom, the Sambo, the Pimp as the historical media constructs of Black men have been identified as the predominant stereotypical presentations that have dominated the photograph, the screen, and the tube for centuries. It is argued that each of these constructs lay the foundation for the contemporary presentation of the thug, which incorporates characteristics of each of the historic images to ground the Black man in criminality. However, many of the works do not place the constructs and the media presentations in any form of social-political context.

As Diawara (1993) points out in his work, *Black American Cinema,* "according to Donald Bogle, there were five basic stereotypes essential to the characterization of Blacks in American films from the very beginning."

Upon exploration of the images, it was found that each image directly relates to productive, hence economic and political shifts that occur within the U.S. These shifts consequently influence the way that Black labor must be exploited. What was found is that each productive shift naturally shifts the focus and direction of the labor—the demand and supply. So just like other races and ethnic groups, the condition and location of Black men in society also shifts. Historically, colonial powers created stereotypical ideologies about Africa, Africans, and African-Americans to support the manner in which it needed to exploit Black labor and Black lands. Consequently, these ideologies had to be redefined to accommodate progressive shifts. While the shifts have been real, the constructions of and presentations of "Blackness" have not been.

THE AGRICULTURAL ERA AND THE BUCK

While many do not care to discuss the continued influence of the institution of enslavement, it is relevant to both historic and contemporary presentations of the Black man in the media. The United States was originally colonized so that the land could be utilized to produce natural resources for the European textile industry. The mass production of natural resources such as cotton allowed the United States to become a major trade port that ultimately led to its wealth accumulation. The production could not have been achieved without the institution of enslavement.

Visually, the Buck, as he has been depicted in some of the most popular historic films such as the infamous *Birth of a Nation* is strong and muscular. His skin is a dark brown, his hair kinky, his features African, and his look and/or expression is wide-eyed, shifty, angry, or wild. He is generally pictured without a shirt and with ripped, torn, and/or dingy pants. He is never fully clothed or dressed in the manner of a gentleman. This image, like the rest, is sensory perceptive. It serves to visually link the Black man to the stereotypical characteristics that were assigned to him—specifically hypersexuality, aggression, savagery, and untrustworthiness. As he is depicted in cinematic classics such as *The Birth of a Nation,* the Buck image is designed to invoke and provoke social fear and mistrust (Spencer, 2005). Diawara (1995) states, "In this film seeking to justify the birth of the Ku Klux Klan, in which Black are all portrayed by Whites in blackface, brutal Black bucks assault White men and rape White women in scenes pretending to recreate Reconstruction's impact on the South . . . No minority was so relentlessly or fiercely typed as the black man" (p. 260).

INDUSTRIALIZATION AND THE UNCLE TOM

While the image of the Buck served to justify the control over the race that was essential to the success of the institution of enslavement, hence, the wealth of this country that was predicated on slave labor, the transition from an agricultural to an industrial economy created a different demand, hence a shift in the labor supply. Several factors, including the political conflict between the North and South, the Civil War and the subsequent signing of the Emancipation Proclamation and the passage of the Thirteenth Amendment influenced a shift in the focus and concentration of labor. First, the conflict between the North and South led the North to make a political power play—the emancipation of African-American people from the institution of slavery, which separated the South from its free labor supply. Further, the onset of the industrial revolution created a need for labor in the industrial sector. These two factors meant that even if they remained segregated, separated, or compartmentalized, Blacks and Whites would have to not only work together but live in close proximity. Consequently, the State had to find ways to replace the intense fear that the Buck image represented and promoted with an image that would promote more tolerance to ensure that Black labor could be utilized in factory and service work with minimal resistance and impact on productivity.

The Uncle Tom construct, as has been historically depicted in the most popular movies and television shows from *Uncle Tom's Cabin, Gone with the Wind, and Tom Sawyer to Shirley Temple,* represents the stereotypes of ignorance, passivity, weakness, and subservience. This image represented a Black man that, contrary to the Buck, could be trusted and did not need to be controlled. Therefore, he was able to work and live within White households and with White women and children without being feared. He was conditioned and trained to automatically acquiesce to white power and privilege and could be counted on to not only control himself but to control members of his race and/or community.

The Postindustrial Era and the Sambo

As technology advances and the mode of production shifts, the need for labor is reduced. The Postindustrial Era or the period that bridges the industrial and the electronic era is significant. It is an era where the U.S. has positioned herself to become a colonial and imperial superpower. She is poised to utilize the promotion of "freedom and democracy" to lure other countries into a capitalist relationship. Internally, the government is working to ensure that the social, political, and infrastructural climate is conducive to such expansion. Roosevelt's New Deal Act was a principle component to preparing and restoring the economy in the post-WW II era. However, increasing racial tensions and the continued overt political oppression and exploitation of African-Americans posed the threat of undermining the nation's expansionist endeavors. Therefore, it was no longer feasible to continue to promote this overt oppression, racism, and exploitation.

The Sambo image is one that emerges in the 1930s and 1940s and is generally seen in both mainstream and all Black cast films, specifically the early works of Director Oscar Micheaux and as recent as films and television shows such as *Meet the Browns* and any film that is directed by Tyler Perry (Spencer 2010). As Wallace proposes in Diawara (1995), "His first appearance occurs on the theatre stage in the minstrel dramas that manufactured White supremacist versions of Black culture . . . This figure was quickly adapted to a set of conventional stereotypes in illustrations, photography, and advertising (p.258). This image represents the stereotypes of ignorance, laziness, intellectual inferiority, irresponsibility, and buffoonery. However, unlike previous images and media interactions where white control and interaction was predominant in the visual presentation of the constructs and characteristics, in the presentation of the Sambo, the Black woman takes on the role of representing "white fear and anger." The Sambo, like the Uncle Tom, represents the emasculated Black man who is incapable of taking on the traditional roles of manhood, i.e., being a provider and protector. However, he is not emasculated by the doings of the White man but by the doings of a masculinized Black woman—the Sapphire (the corresponding Black female construct) who takes on the role of promoting the stereotypes and social sentiments of white society (Spencer, 2010). Collins (2004) argues:

> Under the new racism, these class specific representations of Black masculinity and Black femininity serve several purposes. They speak to the importance that ideologies of class and culture now have in justifying the persistence of racial inequality. Within the universe of these representations, authentic and respectable Black people become constructed as class opposites, and their different cultures help explain why poor and working class Black people are at the bottom of the economic hierarchy, and middle class Black people are not." She furthers, "These class specific images create a Black gender ideology that simultaneously defines Black masculinity and Black femininity in relation to one another and that also positions Black gender ideology as the opposite of normal (White) gender ideology . . . that depicts Black men as being inappropriately weak and Black women as being inappropriately strong" (p. 182).

THE ELECTRONIC ERA, THE WELFARE STATE, AND THE PIMP

The shift from an industrial to an electronic era and the images that emerge during this period must be placed in a historic context in order to understand the sociopolitics that now relate Black men to criminality. The electronic era which preceded the High Tech era in which we now live served to make production more efficient by replacing human labor. As a result of this transition, many lost jobs. In this era, the unemployment rate rose steadily, and the State had to response by expanding the welfare state to include inner postindustrial cities. As the middle class where enjoying the onset of suburbanization, the inner cities were facing an economic crisis.

This era marked a rise in Black films and televisions shows—specifically blaxploitation movies, which introduce the construct of the Pimp. Movies such as *Dolemite, Shaft, Sweet, Sweet Back,* and even more contemporarily *Hustle and Flow*, and later television shows such as *Starsky and Hutch* present Black men as pimps and hustlers. The Pimp constructs introduces the onset of the stereotype of inherent inner city criminality in conjunction with the typical stereotypes of hypersexuality, violence, and aggression. Wallace states that it was not until the "fantastically misogynistic *Sweet Sweetback's Baadasss Song (1971)"* that the "sexually assertive Black males make their way back to the screen (Wallace in Diawara 1995:260). She argues that although this was a highly celebrated independent Black film directed by Melvin Van Peebles that "it goes without saying, however, that practices of resistance are always deeply compromised by their willingness to make major concessions to her hegemonic conventions."

The presentation of his lack of respect for his women, his community, and for the law and authority promote the return of social fear and justify the political aggression against Black leadership that was prominent during that era.

As mentioned above, each of these stereotypical constructs have served the historic purpose of reinforcing stereotypical ideologies about African-American men. Each in their own way and according to the specific eras in which they emerged and dominated mainstream media served to reinforce the inferior placement and subjugation of African-American people. In accordance with both theory and presentation, the media images sought to support the manner in which African-American men needed to be presented in order to promote the acceptance of social hierarchies. And through the historic presentations, one can see how "stereotyped representations of racial minorities in the media have served to represent them as culturally and even genetically inferior" (Doob, 1993:166).

THE INFLUENCE OF THE IMAGES ON PERCEPTION, IMPRESSION, AND AFFECT CONTROL

The sociopolitical and historic foundation of the presentation of Black men in the media is clear. Each is a direct construction that serves to visually promote the stereotypes of the race. The stereotypical constructions of the images of Black men goes back centuries and have therefore become not only engrained in the fiber of American culture but in the minds and psyche of the American people. Therefore, as Eberhardt (2008) argued, they are not images that can easily be deconstructed. Many do not understand the relevance and the significance of the relationship between sensory experiences, cognitive association, perception, and affect control. However, understanding the manner in which the psyche receives, processes, and recalls information both consciously and subconsciously is important to truly understanding the magnitude of the problem of how Black men have historically and continue to be presented in the media. Understanding the theoretical influence of perception development, impression, and affect is crucial to understanding the negative implications of the contemporary presentation of the criminal construct of Black men that is promoted in the media.

Most often, as a result of the history of separatism, and the pattern of migrating to those like us, people do not extend their social and familial experiences beyond their race. The work environment may be multiracial, multiethnic, and multicultural, but when the work day is over, most retreat to segregated communities or enclaves of the community where interracial interaction is limited. Therefore, one must question how people derive their perception of other races. The history of racial prejudice between Blacks and other races, segregation, exclusion, and oppression has created a stigma around the Black race that further lends to the consistent lack of interracial experiences.

As a result, the media as a form of mass communication is one of the most common and prevalent ways in which people gain their understanding of other races and cultural experiences. So when the presentations that are contrived to promote and manipulate social perception are consistently negative, how can one expect the masses to develop and embrace alternate perceptions?

Theoretically, the concept of sensory perception is centered on the way in which individuals use their senses to shape their subjective realities. Each sense, specifically the visual and auditory senses which are arguably the most powerful, creates a sensory experience that individuals define and assign meaning or value to. These values and meanings are then correlated with/to the image and "logged" into our brains. This interaction subsequently guides the way that we define and perceive events, phenomena, images, etc. As George Herbert Mead and Charles Horton Cooley illustrate in their theories on the development of self, perceptions shape the way that individuals view and experience the world. And we, as individuals and then collectives, become the product of our collective experiences (Macionis, 2007).

This concept extends from psychology to principles of reasoning. Psychologically, once an image is assigned a value or a value is assigned an image, either will invoke a recall of the other. So if Black men are associated a value of criminality, then the image of a Black man will automatically invoke a recall of the value of criminality, and the value of criminality will automatically invoke a recall of the image of a Black man. Conversely, even by the principles of reasoning formula—if A=B and B=C, then A=C. Therefore, by association, if a *Black man* represents a *savage or a criminal*. And *savages and criminals* are to be *feared or despised*. Then the *Black man* is to be *feared or despised*.

So in analyzing the influence of the presentation of Black men in the media, one cannot negate that when the visual presentation of an object/ image is linked to a specific value, if repeated, internalized, and in the absence of alternative presentations or value assignments that give the mind an option, the visual presentation will automatically invoke *an* association to the assigned value and subsequently generate the emotion and/or sentiment attached to that value. When the presentation of homogenous images becomes the normative presentation of a group, that presentation becomes the identification of the collective and not just the individual. Consequently, by association, as Gestalt theory would suggest, the visual presentation of the Black man in the media becomes a representation and identification of the whole (or totality) of the Black male identity and experience. It subsequently becomes difficult to separate fiction (images and actors) from fact (the reality of the heterogeneity of the human experience), and so the fiction becomes the fact or the reality.

For Black men, this poses a great problem. The thug or gangsta' image is the homogenous presentation of Black male identity. It is an image, however, that is taken from the urban cultural and style of presentation, which includes the way in which Black men wear their hair, clothes, walk, talk, greet, etc. Just like any other subculture that is guided by race, ethnicity, age, class, gender, sexuality, and even religion, the urban/inner city subculture is distinct and, like others, differs or deviates from traditional cultural codes. So when an entire cultural appearance becomes symbolic of criminality, it criminalizes all who embrace it. Therefore, in order to shed the association or value, Black men must conform to traditional and/or dominant codes in order to be accepted. To avoid or present an alternative to the value of criminality, the Black man must, as an example, cut his hair, shave, wear traditional, conservative, and/or socially acceptable clothing; he must give up his dialect and his cultural rituals. He must deny his "swagger."

THE CONTEMPORARY MEDIA IMAGE OF THE THUG, CRIME, AND THE PRISON INDUSTRIAL COMPLEX

The High Tech and Global Era, as Marx predicted, creates a shift in the labor force that increases the surplus labor pool because of the shrinking labor market. While technology and globalization has its benefits, it also has its perils. The most significant of the perils is the negative effect that it has on the labor market in the United States. While technology makes communication and trade more efficient, it also facilitates production, which means that it replaces human labor. In communication, it replaces the operator, the telemarketer, the customer service representative. In correspondence, it replaces the postal worker; in banking, it replaces the lower level representatives in the banking industry; and in retail, it replaces the cashier. This combined with globalization, which includes the ability to "outsource," which allows corporations to take advantage of more lax labor laws and wage labor relationships by utilizing labor outside of the United States, also adversely effects the American labor market. Even Wilson, as far back as 1978, recognized the impact that the transition from the industrial to the high-tech economy was having on the labor force. In his work, he argued:

> *In one interpretation of the relationship between joblessness and structural changes in the economy, Charles C. Killingsworth maintains . . . there has been a long run decline in the demand for low skilled, poorly educated workers and a long run rise in the demand for high skilled, well-educated workers, and that this twist has proceeded farther and faster than adjustments in the supply of labor, resulting in an imbalance in the labor market"* (Wilson, 1978:95).

As a result, the compression of the labor pool that occurs because of a reduction in the need for human labor forces those who once occupied the surplus labor positions, which include lower level service positions into unemployment. The higher the rate of unemployment in the era of neo liberalism, the greater the "social burden" to address the needs of those who are unemployed becomes. Wilson even argues that "one of the consequences in the rise of new poverty neighborhoods has been the souring of race relations. The problems associated with high joblessness and declining social organization in inner city ghetto neighborhoods are *perceived* to spill over into other parts of the city (Wilson 1996:183).

The political and economic reality of an experience that is core to most working class people who once derived their income from industrial labor is once again narrowed to or focused on the African-American male. Therefore, the fear of the backlash that authors such as Hacker

(1995) illustrated encourages the perception of "the likelihood of Black criminality" that is supported by the new image of the "thug."

In accordance with the effect of the economy on inner city Black men is the relationship to presentations that promote deviance, the thirteenth amendment, laws, and policing policies that target inner city communities, and the benefit of the Prison Industrial Complex as a form of free labor. Visually, as represented by virtually every popular mainstream rap artist, such as 50 Cent, Lil Wayne, the "thug image" looks angry and violent. Not only does he rap about murder, criminality, and his sexual exploits, but he is almost always pictured without a shirt, his chest and arms adorned with tattoos, his hair braided, locked, or covered by a doo rag or a hood that covers his face. He is pictured armed with guns and associated with drugs. Therefore, the association to the value of criminality and violence is without question. The stereotype is further legitimized by the fact that the rap artist themselves voluntarily present this role and character even when it is not true to who they themselves really are. To compound the urban presentation, the oversaturation of Black criminality that is found on crime reality television shows—that includes shows such as *Peoples Court, Judge Mathis, Judge Joe Brown, Bait Car, Cops, The First 48, Crime 360, Cold Case,* fictional crime shows that include every *Law and Order* and all of the *CSIs,* and the overrepresentation of Black criminality in the news media—add immensely to the issue.

Criminals and murderers, understandably so, are to be feared. So all Black men, especially those who look like the presentations that rap artist and Black male actors are forced to portray, are to be feared. Socially and politically, although the criminality may be confined to the inner city, it becomes a social and political issue. So to avoid an escalation of "the problem" of Black criminality, that has now become a collective reality in the minds of those who have limited to no contact with Black men or the inner city, the problem—Black men must be managed. But not just some or a few Black men but all Black men because it is argued that in the American psyche because of the homogenous media presentations of criminality, there is no separation or heterogeneity in the Black male experience. The presentation of the few represents the whole. Even scholars and authors reflect the assertion. For example, bestselling author Hatcher (1995), on one hand states:

> *What most Americans regard as "black crime" has become a preoccupation of the public and private life. Black men and the offenses they commit are viewed differently from other felons and felonies (p.184).*

But goes on to state:

> *Very many blacks who are young and poor feel they have never had a fair chance, nor do they see that prospect changing. In light of the insults and discrimination they have faced throughout their lives, it is not surprising that as many as do vent their resentment in violence. Through crime, blacks are paying whites back in the most ominous way they can (p.194).*

This does not negate the notion that Black men are a homogenous group and experience the world differently but only justifies the stereotypical presentation by blaming Black men's criminality on racism.

Once again, the Black man is to be feared, hence controlled or now even annihilated. Some may argue that the statement may seem like a conspiracy theory. But who complains when a Black man is arrested, beaten, or even murdered by the police or some ordinary white citizen who had a justifiable reason to fear—he was Black? Al Sharpton? There is rarely widespread social outcry that crosses racial and cultural lines, much less national media exposure that would allow society to know and understand the frequency of such events.

Not only do the consequences of the media presentation of Black men as "criminals" effect social perception, but it also affects laws and legislation and the balance of policing and sentencing. As Hacker (1995) states:

> After the end of slavery, the nation found it expedient to maintain Blacks as a subordinate caste. But given their admission to citizenship, new controls had to be devised to keep them in place. One was to give the police a long leash,

devising ways to absolve them if they went too far with their powers (p.194).

The constant portrayal of Black men as criminal, violent, deviant thugs in the media has its effects. It serves to create a perception that those presentations are accurate representations of Black men in society. From the news to crime and reality television to urban media's very own portrayal of Black men in this manner, all serve to reinforce and/or even promote the notion of Black criminality. In such, the collective social affect is shifted from that of understanding that like all other races, Black men are not a homogenous racial group that are predestined to be criminal by their biological makeup, as theorists such as Lombroso would suggest, but a multidimensional group of individuals that will be shaped by their subjective experiences, even those that occur in urban areas. As Eberhardt et al. (2008) suggest, "The findings show that society is more likely to condone violence against black criminal suspects as a result of its broader inability to accept African-Americans as fully human" (Eberhardt et al., 2008).

However, contrary to the oversaturation of images of Black male criminality that are presented in the media, further research that investigates the validity of racialized crime "reality" television shoes, specifically the work of Monk-Turner et al. (2007), found that the racial and gendered dynamics found in crime television shows actually deviated from the Uniform Crime Report (UCR) for the same incidents. They found that in shows such as *COPS*, white males were more likely to be overrepresented as officers, whereas Black men were more likely to be overrepresented as offenders (Monk-Turner et al., 2001:3). More consequentially though was their finding that most people are more likely to ground their understanding of crime from these shows rather than actual experience and or research. According the study:

Carmody (1998), Fishman (1999), and Kappeler et al. (1996) have argued that crime-based reality television reinforces myths of crime and law enforcement. The primary myth is that black men commit more crime than others, which leads to fears of being victimized by African-American men (see Oliver and Armstrong, 1998; Robinson, 2000). Crime-based television programming does not aim to educate the general public about criminological and sociological theoretical understandings of crime causation which are based on the recognition that crime is not primarily the result of *crazed individuals (Monk-Turner et al., 2007:5).*

The problem with the media presentations is that when a collective fear that is generated by misrepresentations that are identified as "reality" guide social perception, "real life" Black men in society become subjected to the consequence of that fear. Sean Bell was an unarmed man who was coming from his bachelor's party at a local night club in New York. Suspected of soliciting a prostitute and then perceived to be armed, he was fired upon fifty-one times. This is an example of the consequences of stereotypically constructed affect and perception. Amadou Diallo was an unarmed man who looked like a rape suspect. He was fired upon forty-one times. This is an example of the consequences of stereotypically constructed affect and perception. Ousmane Zongo was unarmed. He wasn't suspected of any crime but was shot four times in the back. This is an example of the consequences of stereotypically constructed affect and perception. Or most recently, the case of seventeen-year-old Jordan Miles, an honor student and violinist, was beaten by Pittsburgh Police for carrying a bottle of mountain dew in his pocket. The police believed the bottle of soda to be a gun. And then there are not so clean cases where the Castle Doctrine extends the right to be the enforcers to ordinary citizens and be protected under the law without investigation and or prosecution. Like the case of Bobby L. Gadsden Jr., a twenty-one-year-old young man who allegedly broke into the home of his friend and was shot in the back of the head by his friend's father as he ran out of the back door. These are the most significant examples of how stereotypically constructed images of Black criminality manifest in affect and perception.

"Justice" as an objective reality is shaped by the subjective reality of those who judge. Judicial officers, police, attorneys, etc., are not privileged to some other information or presentations that the masses are not. Many who are products of middle and upper class families have limited personal experiences with the Black race and urban settings. The level of segregation and the lack of interracial experiences are compounded in Southern and Midwestern states. Consequently, like the rest of society, authority figures shape their perceptions through the media too, and their perceptions become validated by the disproportionate minority contact with the criminal justice system.

The officers in the case of Diallo and Bell were acquitted of any wrongdoing. In spite of the fact that most would consider the murder of each "overkill" especially if the victim where a twenty-two-year-old white mother who was due to be married the next morning or a twenty-year-old white woman going into her home in the suburbs. The officer in the case of Zongo was sentenced to probation and five hundred hours community service which would be an insult if the victim had been a nineteen-year-old White Harvard student who was suspected of nothing. The officers in the case of Miles are on "paid leave" pending an investigation. And the question must be asked. How would society react if the victim had been a sixteen-year-old White girl with the exact same credentials as Miles? And finally, Moncks Corner Police Department vehemently refused to investigate or charge Mr. Barwick, the homeowner who killed Bobby L. Gadsden Jr.; it was ruled justifiable at the scene. Again, what if Mr. Gadsden was a twenty-one-year-old white girl who just got caught up with the wrong crowd? Not only do Black men become victims of assault and murder, their lives become meaningless in the eyes of social and moral justice. In essence, the fear that invoked the murder of the victims justifies the officers and citizens responses and actions. And so while in the eyes of justice now, the officers and citizens become victims of that fear; the lives of Black men become mere "casualties of war," "matter of fact" losses that lose more meaning with each situation.

Racially, a Black man invokes a degree of fear that is far more elevated than a White woman. Therefore, the responses to a White woman will be different than the responses to a Black man. The officers' fear, defense, and training justified the action in the eyes of the law and justice—in spite of the circumstances. Why? Because the judicial system is headed by judges (who are merely men and women who take on the role of judging) whose perceptions are shaped in the same manner as the rest of society.

If those who run the systems have limited contact with Black men or the inner city, then the same stereotypical presentations become the foundation for how they develop their perceptions. While it may be argued that justice is blind, the truth is that men see and feel. While it may be argued that justice is supposed to be objective, the truth is that men are not; they measure by their experience and capacity to understand. Again, we are all products of our experiences. We do not perceive outside of the scope of our experiences. Our interactions and judgments are based on those experiences and perceptions. Therefore, justice is, by no means, blind. The eyes of justice have the capacity to be tainted by the subjective interpretation and perception of the men and women who "rule." It was argued:

> While the Diallo Decision was shocking in 2000, the Bell Decision, in 2008, as heart crushing as it may have been, was not. As a matter of fact, any other decision would have been far more shocking than *this* full acquittal. Why? Because by *not* convicting the officers of *any* of the charges, the Judge in this case not only "ruled" the officers' use of force—firing 51 shots—against this group of unarmed "men of color" justifiable, but more significantly the Judge's decision reflected his own sentiment, belief, and agreement that the officers' actions were grounded in their perception and judgment that the men, who they *assumed/perceived* to be "armed and dangerous," indeed posed a threat (Spencer 2010).

As Monk-Turner et al. (2007) support the media presentations reinforce the notion that members of society will be victimized by Black men and consequently justify fear and its consequences. Based on their findings, they surmised:

> If televised images on crime-based reality television shape the public perception of who commits crime, as well as what types of crime they tend to commit, then reality television is doing a poor job relating the facts. If one based their understanding of crime, law, and law enforcement on reality television, one would believe that virtually all police officers are white men. They would also believe that black men committed most crimes as well as the most serious ones (Monk-Turner et al., 2007:11).

The image of the evil Black man in the dark alley waiting to rob, rape, beat, or murder has been an image that has loomed in the American psyche for centuries. While many may argue that these presentations have minimal consequences, as illustrated, they have consequences not just for the interaction between the races and the ability of the nation to truly overcome the barriers of race and racial fear, but it has implications to the quality of life and justice for Black men who are increasingly being affected by the media presentations that link them to criminality.

CONCLUSION

There is a direct correlation between images, perception, and affect control. It involves the use of the media as a means of shaping and manipulating public perception and thereby controlling social and collective affect. The media, as a tool of mass communication, represents the most common and widespread means of promoting images and disseminating information. The manner in which the images are presented and the meanings that are attached to the images serve the direct and indirect function of shaping the way that people view, interpret, and develop their subjective realities. When the media has been identified as a tool of manipulating presentations in order to secure conformity to social, political, economic, and/or expansionist endeavors, not only should the patterns of homogenous and unilateral presentations be questioned, but so should the agenda of those who control the presentations.

The history of oppression and exploitation that surrounds the introduction of African-American men to this country should not be negated. The stereotypes that were used to justify the enslavement of the race—that have never been undone—cannot be dismissed from discourse about the manner in which Black men are presented and perceived in contemporary media and the American psyche today. The race card is not a card; it is a reality that has shaped and continues to shape the social perception about an entire group of people. Therefore, it must not be reduced as a contributing factor in the analysis of crime and media.

Is it fair for young Black men to have to neglect and negate their own cultural expressions to remove themselves from unfairly imposed stigmas? Is it fair for the lives of Black men to be taken simply to accommodate a police officer's or an everyday citizen's misperception of fear? Is it fair to continue to mask stereotypes about the group as realities in order to continue to justify racial prejudice, oppression, and exploitation? Or is it fair to continue to allow the media to oversaturate the world with stereotypes when they are not factually grounded and accurate representations of the group?

Black men represent a social collective that is comprised of a multitude of different characters and characteristics, just like any other race and ethnic group. While Gestalt emphasizes the whole, the race and gender of "Black men" is the sum of its parts. It is a heterogeneous, not a homogenous group who have both shared distinct experiences and histories. When the Black man as a collective is criminalized, it is not innocent or without consequence. It threatens the freedom, equality, inclusion, interaction, quality of life, and life itself for all Black men.

As a result of historically grounded stigmatization, ostracism, separation, exploitation, and oppression, the Black man has endured a history of discrimination, exclusion, beatings, burnings, physical and psychological castration and abuse, and murder. The manner in which perceptions about Black men have been developed and promoted have served as a major accomplice to the brutality by forcing the lack of empathy and understanding that is rooted in the presentation and perpetuation of historic stereotypes that have justified racism, enslavement, discrimination and exclusion, and generated public fear of Black men for centuries.

References

Berberoglu, B. 1998. "An Introduction to Classical and Contemporary Social Theory: A Critical Perspective" 2nd ed. General Hall. Dix Hills NY.

Bogle, T. (2003). Toms, Coons, Mulattoes, Mammies and Bucks.

Collins, P. (2004). *Black Sexual Politics.* Routledge Press. N.Y, NY.

Davis, A. (1999). *The Prison Industrial Complex.* AK Press. Oakland, CA.

Diawara, M. (1993). *Black American Cinema.* Routledge Press. NY. NY.

Doob, C. (1993). "Racism: An American Cauldron." Harper Collins Publishers Inc. New York, NY.

Eberhardt, J. (2008). "Not Yet Human: Implicit Knowledge, Historical Dehumanization, and Contemporary Consequences." Journal of Personality and Social Psychology. http://news.stanford.edu/pr/2008/pr-eber-021308.html

Gomes, R., Williams, L. (1995). "From Exclusion to Inclusion: The Long Struggle for African-American Political Power." Connecticut. Praeger Press.

Gunther, L. (1982). "Black Image: European Eyewitness Accounts of Afro-American Life." National University Press. Port Washington, NY.

Hacker, A. (1995). "Two Nations: Black and White, Separate, Hostile, Unequal." Ballantine Books. NY, NY

Hassan, T. (2001). "Gendered Visions." Africa World Press. New Jersey

Monk-Turner, E., Martinez, H. Holbrook, J, and Harvey, N. (2007). "Are Reality Television Crime Shows Continuing to Perpetuate Crime Myths?" Internet Journal of Criminology. www.internetjournalofcriminology.com/Monk-Turner.

Spencer, Z. (2005): "A Historical Materialist Analysis of the Visual Presentation of the African-American Woman in Mainstream Film 1896-2004." Dissertation. Washington DC. Proquest

Spencer, Z. (2011). "Murda, Misogyny, and Mayhem: Hip Hop, Media, and the Culture of Abnormality in the Urban Community." University Press. Lanham MD

Wallace, M. (1978). "Black Macho and the Myth of the Superwoman." NY, NY. Dial Press.

Wilson, W.J. (1996). "When Work Disappears: The World of the New Urban Poor." Random House Press, New York, NY.

Wilson, W.J. (1978). "The Declining Significance of Race." Random House Press. New York. NY.

Zeitlin, E. (1997). *Ideology and the Development of Sociological Theory*, 6th Ed. Theoretical Perspectives in Sociology. Prentice Hall. New York, NY.

The Human Cost of Malaria Infections in a Developing Society: An Examination of Selected Households in Maiduguri Metropolis

David Irefin, Kogi State University,
Steve Metiboba, Kogi State University,
Babajidda Mallah, University of Maiduguri

ABSTRACT

Malaria is a major disease burden in most developing countries of the world—Nigeria inclusive. Its adverse impact on socioeconomic life in these countries can no longer be in doubt. This study is aimed at estimating the human cost of malaria infection on selected households in Maiduguri, capital city of Borno State in the North eastern geographical zone of Nigeria. One hundred twenty-five respondents were interviewed for this study, cutting across business men/women, civil servants, and students' social strata. The primary source of data for the study was obtained through the use of questionnaire administration and oral interview. Secondary data such as hospital records, journals, and health periodicals were also employed in the study. Descriptive statistics including simple frequency distributions, mean, mode, and the likes were used to analyze the data generated in the study. Findings from the study revealed, among others, that the cost of malaria in monetary terms in the study area is relatively very high, as an average individual spends up to N5,000 per month on the malaria parasite. This paper recommends that government at all levels should embark on intensive and extensive awareness campaign for her citizenry and reintroduce aerial spray of insecticides as these can drastically lead to a reduction in the incidence of people getting in contact with mosquitoes, the perceived causal agent of malaria disease. This can greatly prevent the people from coming in contact with mosquitoes, hence reduction in cases of malaria.

Introduction

Background of the Study

Malaria is one of the most severe public health problems worldwide, affecting almost every aspect of the economy. It is among the leading cause of death. World Health Organization (WHO) estimates that over three hundred million cases of malaria arise every year with approximately two to three million deaths (WHO, 2002). The impact of malaria has been felt from time immemorial to date. Its impact on human productivity, household, as well as national income, has been felt or seen through low productivity, high mortality rate, and low standard of living. The disease is a major health problem in Nigeria with even transmission throughout the country. It accounts for about 50 percent of outpatient consultation, 15 percent of hospital admission, and also prime among the top three causes of death in the country (NMCPA, 1996-2001). More importantly, it is a social and economic problem, which consumes about 3.5 million U.S. dollars in government funding in various control attempts in 2001 (WHO, 2002).

The economic impact of malaria in Nigeria cannot be overemphasized. Malaria has impacted so much on the Nigerian economy. It is one of the four leading causes of mortality among infants, children, and adults. It is estimated that it is responsible for about 25 percent mortality in infants, 30 percent in children, and 11 percent maternal mortality in Nigeria.

According to Sajay (2000), about 50 percent of the population of Nigeria experience malaria infection each year. Malaria also contributes to both poverty and underdevelopment in Nigeria through reduced productivity and absenteeism from work. According to Onwujekwe and Okonkwo (2000), malaria has a demographic effect on the Nigerian economy, as people's decision on where to live, work, or reside are significantly affected by their propensity/vulnerability to malaria infection. It has also been stated that poverty is equally a significant reason or cause for the high level of malaria in Nigeria.

There have been several attempts at eradicating malaria in Nigeria; among such attempts are Rollback Malaria program, workshops conducted by WHO, and other governmental and nongovernmental health agencies. These attempts have proven to be inadequate as the problems of malaria are still present around us, especially in economic terms. This informs the reason for this study.

STATEMENT OF THE PROBLEM

Malaria is an endemic disease that is taking heavy toll on Africa and other developing countries in the world. In many of these regions, the burden of malaria has been increasing even further in recent years. When measured in economic terms, the cost of malaria is enormous. A careful examination of relevant literature on this study reveals that highly malaria-infected countries are among the poorest in the world and typically have low economic growth rates; some, to an extent, have experienced decline in the standard of living of its citizenry in the past thirty years. Malaria has played a significant role in the poor economic performance of these countries. Malaria imposes a heavy cost not only on the current income of a country but also its rate of economic growth and therefore on its level of economic development in the long run. It is in view of the above that this paper attempts to estimate the human cost of malaria on selected households in Maiduguri.

OBJECTIVES OF THE STUDY

The main objective of this paper, therefore, is to examine the human cost of malaria infection among selected households in Maiduguri metropolis. The specific objectives of the study are to:

Examine the effects of malaria on the productivity of households; Determine the labor hours lost to malaria in the study area; and

Determine the monetary value of the labor hours lost to malaria infection on the households in the study area.

RESEARCH QUESTIONS

The paper provides answers to the following questions:

What are the major effects of malaria on productivity in the study area? How much labor hours were lost to the scourge of malaria in the study area? How much, in monetary terms, was lost to the infection of malaria in the study area for the period under study?

LITERATURE REVIEW

MALARIA AND THE GLOBAL ECONOMY

Malaria impacts on the world so much that it is becoming a source of concern to health organizations, economists, sociologists, and other concerned individuals and organizations. According to Foster (1998), when a person gets infected, he gets sick. The person gets sick for a period of several weeks. He doesn't work, he doesn't take care of his family, and he just struggles to survive and live through it. Now, this has very huge economic consequences for both the individual and the economy at large. According to him, those countries with high level of endemic malaria and other tropical diseases have much slower economic growth than countries with low level of endemicity.

Malaria and poverty are intimately related/connected. Countries with intensive malaria had income levels in 1995 of only 33 percent than that of countries without malaria, whether or not the country is in Africa. According to him, the high incidence of malaria on poor countries is mainly a consequence of poverty. The distribution and intensity of the disease is primarily determined by the ecological conditions, which support the malaria mosquito vector.

In the most endemic regions like Gambia, Sudan, Malawi, and Zambia, efforts to eliminate malaria has been effective in countries that have succeeded in eliminating the scourge or substantially. Five years after eliminating malaria in their economies, these countries have experienced higher economic growth than their neighbors.

According to Foster (1998), about 5 percent of deaths worldwide among children are due to malaria. The burden is much greater in sub-Saharan Africa, with 15 percent of all disability-adjusted life years (DALYS) lost to malaria. According to him, an estimated US$180 million are spent annually on both direct cost of productivity, time lost, and other indirect cost and other losses.

According to a report by Role Back malaria (2001), malaria kills over one million people worldwide every year, and most of these preventable deaths are among African productive labor force. Despite efforts at combating malaria, it continues to account for 90 percent of under five mortality in Africa and constitutes 10 percent of the continents overall disease burden. Malaria causes 30-50 percent of in-patient admissions, incurs 40 percent of total public health expenditure, and up to 50 percent of out-patient visits hospitals and medical centers for follow-up management.

Annual economic growth rate in countries with high malaria transmission over a period of twenty-five years were 1.3 percent lower than in non-malarious countries. A poor family living in malaria-infected areas may spend up to 25 percent or more of its annual income on prevention and treatment of malaria. Malaria has slowed economic growth in African countries by 1.3 percent per year. As a result of the compounded effects over thirty-five years, the ADP level for African countries now 32 percent lower than it would have been in the absence of malaria.

World Health Organization (WHO, 1997) estimated that there are fifty million cases of malaria each year. It has been hypothesized that a three-degree-Celsius coverage covering warming of the planet would increase the incidence of this disease by 10-15 percent. Also, some preventive measures, such as restriction of green house gas emissions, which exacerbated poverty and public health would be placed at greater risk since wealth tends to bring health and longevity, poverty tends to bring infectious diseases, high infant and childhood mortality, and short lifespan. Thus, some of these malaria-preventive policies put pressure on the economic power of the people, making them poorer and thus exposed to disease (David 1997).

According to Centre for International Development, Harvard University, the London school of hygiene and tropical medicine, high malarious countries are among the very poorest in the world and typically have very low rates of economic growth. Many have experienced outright decline in living standards in the past thirty years. Malaria has played a significant role in the poor economic performance of these countries.

The annual loss of growth from malaria in malaria-endemic countries is estimated to range as high as 1.3 percent per year. If this loss is compounded for fifteen years, the GNP level in the fifteen years is reduced by nearly a fifth and the toll on countries to mount with time. This is known as short-term costs. These short-run lost which among other things are loss of work time, economic losses associated with loss of productive labor force, child mortality, and the costs of treatment and prevention are typically to be higher than one percent of a country's gross national product.

These estimates, however, neglect many other short-run costs. For insolence, very new studies include the economic cost of the pain and suffering associated with the increase in the prevalence of the disease, yet researchers found out that households are to bear the direct income loss caused by malaria in order to minimize its effects. That is that the pain, suffering, and uncertainty associated with the disease is very high and should be included among its short-term costs.

Apart from these short-run costs, malaria also impedes economic growth and development through its effects on flow of trade and foreign investment and commerce.

Repeated effects of malaria may affect a child's physical and cognitive development and may reduce a child's attendance and performance at school. Furthermore, repeated bouts of malaria may expose individuals to chronic malnutrition, anemia and increased vulnerability to other diseases.

Malaria may have adverse effects and demographic consequences. Malaria subsequently raises the chances of labor force mortality. The investment which households can afford to make in the well-being of each infected family member is limited. These leads to reduction in the average level of health care and education per child.

According to Roll Back Malaria (2001), the annual economic growth in countries with high malaria transmission has historically been lower than in countries without malaria. Economists believe that malaria is responsible for a growth penalty of up to 1.3 percent per year in some African countries. When compounded over the years, this leads to substantial difference in GDP between countries with and without malaria.

Furthermore, Roll Back Malaria (2001) states that the presence of malaria in a community or country also hampers individuals and national prosperity because of its influence on social and economic decisions. The risk of contracting malaria in endemic areas can deter investments both internal and external and affects individual and household decision making in many ways that have negative impact on economic productivity and growth.

Malaria is hurting the living standard of Africans and also preventing the improvement of living standards of future generations. Malaria-free countries average three times higher GDP per person than malarious countries. (Press Release WHO 28:2000).

According to Samba (2001), the social and economic consequences of malaria in any region are very grave. It is a major contributing factor to poverty. According to him, it keeps many adults from work and many children from school. In 1997 alone, according to health economists, the African countries lost more than two billion U.S. dollars because of malaria and malaria related diseases.

Malaney (2003) did a research to assess the economic burden of malaria by means of a cross-country regression analysis. It was found out that the disease is a significant factor in long-term economic growth and development.

Evaluating the burden of malaria can be approached in two ways—the direct costs and indirect cost using the cost of illness (COI) method. The direct costs are private as well as nonprivate medical care costs. Private cost includes private expenditure on prevention, diagnosis, treatment, and follow-up management. These would be expenses as those required for bed nets, doctor's fees, the cost of antimalaria drugs, and transportation to medical facilities and necessary support for the patients. Nonprivate medical care costs include public expenditure on preventive and treatment of the resulting disease.

METHODOLOGY

DESCRIPTION OF THE STUDY AREA

Maiduguri is the capital city of Borno State in the North Eastern geographical zone of Nigeria. It lies at the centre of Borno State and has an estimated population of about 1,096,589 and has population density of 42 inhabitants per square kilometer (census 2006). It is boarded in the North-East by Jere Local government area and on the south by Konduga local government area respectively. On the West, it is boarded by Magumeri local government area.

Maiduguri can be accessible through three major modes of transportation; these are: By air, road and railway.

Maiduguri has an international airport and has a regular flight to Abuja, Lagos and Yola among others. At present, Maiduguri is served by the IRS, Arik among others. Maiduguri international Airport also serves as one of the airports used in Hajj operations.

Maiduguri is accessible to all the states of the Federation by road; Maiduguri has a link of roads that links it to major cities in the country,

Akwa Ibom, Aba, Onitsha through Jos. Also it is linked to Lagos, Ibadan through Kano. Maiduguri is also accessible to all the various local governments in the state; such as Baga, Bama, Kaga, Konduga, Magumeri, etc,. Also neighboring countries of Niger, Chad and Cameroun can also be easily reached by road through Baga and Michika, etc.

There is a railway terminus situated in Maiduguri. This railroad links Maiduguri town to major cities like, Lagos and Port Harcourt. This railroad pass through Bauchi, Oturkpo, Kafanchan, Enugu, Aba to Port Harcourt. It also passes through Kano to Lagos, but because of present failure and poor railroads, the accessibility to Maiduguri on railroads ceased for quite some time now.

CLIMATE AND VEGETATION

Maiduguri has a climate which is hot and dry for a greater part of the year. The period of rainy season is influenced by some factors such as the directions of the rain-bearing winds and topography of the area. In general, the raining season is normally between the months of June to September with relative humidity of about 49 percent and evaporation of 203 millimeter per year.

Maiduguri is infected by many mosquitoes throughout the year. Mosquitoes breed easily on the neem trees, unkept swage, refuse dumps, and dirty environment.

OCCUPATION AND TRIBE

A large percentage of the population in Maiduguri are predominantly farmers and business men and women. With a very large percentage of farmers, it takes an agrarian society in nature with millet, maize, sorghum, gum Arabic, and groundnuts being the major produce. Maiduguri is also home to fishermen, which is one of the major occupations of the people, especially during the rainy season. Maiduguri has one big river that passes through the center of the town. This river is a major source of fishing especially during the wet season. Maiduguri is also becoming a very busy commercial town with trading and business activities growing by day.

Maiduguri is inhabited predominantly by the Kanuri. It is also inhabited by other ethnic groups like Hausa, Bura, Higi, Shuwa, Fulani, and the likes. Other nation-states and languages such as the Igbo, Yorubas, Tivs, Idoma, Igala, and a host of others from other parts of Nigeria also live in Maiduguri town.

SOURCES OF DATA

The primary data were obtained through the use of questionnaire administration and oral interview where necessary. The secondary data were obtained from research works conducted by numerous scholars, hospital records, journals, and health periodicals.

TECHNIQUE OF DATA ANALYSIS

Descriptive statistics was employed in analyzing the data. Descriptive statistics shows general patterns of events of a distribution using known parameters such as mean, mode, simple percentages, tables, skewness, range, or through the use of symbols.

The choice of descriptive statistics is a result of the nature of data obtained. The data is not complex enough for sophisticated statistical tools to be applied.

DATA PRESENTATION AND ANALYSIS AND INTERPRETATION

One hundred fifty subjects were given questionnaires to elicit relevant information on the study. One hundred twenty-five respondents were eventually used for this descriptive survey. Twenty-five questionnaires administered to the targeted population were not turned in. This nonresponse constituted less than 17 percent of the total study population. The response rate was considered significant enough to proceed on the study.

Table 1: Frequency Distribution of Respondents

Categories	Frequency	Percentage (%)
Business	60	48
Civil servants	40	32
Students	25	20
Total	125	100

Source: Field Survey, 2011.

From Table 1, it was discovered that sixty respondents (48 percent of the sampled population) were business men/women and forty respondents (32 percent) were civil servants, while twenty-five respondents (20 percent) were students.

Table 2: Sex Distribution of Respondents

Categories	Frequency	Percentage (%)
Male	75	60
Female	50	40
Total	125	100

Source: Field Survey, 2011.

Table 2 shows that 60 percent of the study population were males, while the rest (40 percent) were females.

Table 3: Trend and Prevalence of Malaria in Maiduguri Metropolis

Year	Total Patients tested	Malaria Positive	Malaria Negative	% Malaria Prevalence
2005	18,683	13,030	5,653	-
2006	19,112	13,801	5,311	7.71
2007	19,985	18,756	1,229	49.55
2008	28,754	23,874	4,880	51.18
2009	30,145	24,960	5,185	10.86
2010	45,849	40,132	5,717	71.72
Total	162,528	134,553	27,975	

Source: Authors' Field Survey, 2011.

From Table 3, it can be seen that the trend of malaria infection has been increasing progressively. This ranges from 13,030 cases in 2005 to 40,132 cases in 2010. The rate of the number of those tested positive to malaria has been on the increase at an alarming rate. As shown in Table 3, the prevalence of malaria infection increases from 7.71 percent in 2006 to 49.555 percent in 2007. This increased to 51.18 percent in 2008 which later reduced to 10.86 percent in 2009. But this reduction was short lived as in 2010, the percentage jumped to an alarming rate of 71.72 percent. If this is not checked, the impact of malaria in the metropolis will be enormous in the most foreseeable future. A total number of 162,526 people were tested between the years 2005 and 2010. Out of these, 134,553 were tested positive, while 27,975 were tested negative. The inference is that malaria is becoming an endemic disease in the study area.

FREQUENCY OF INFECTION

From Table 4, twenty-two respondents (28.95 percent) said they received treatment on regular basis. While forty-eight respondents (63.16 percent) said that it is not too often that they receive treatment. The remaining six respondents (7.87 percent) said they do not receive malaria treatment.

Table 4: Frequency of Infection

Categories	Frequency	Percentage (%)
On regular basis	48	38.4
Not too often	65	52.0
No idea	12	9.6
Total	125	100

Source: Field Survey, 2011.

Table 4 shows that 38.4 percent of the respondents said that malaria attacks them frequently, while 52.0 percent of the respondents said that malaria attacks them not too frequently. This may be a result of inadequate treatment or a result of inadequate preventive measures. Lack of proper awareness campaign, illiteracy, and ignorance of some people, inadequate equipment in most hospitals, inadequate trained personnel, as well as poor sanitary conditions, have further aggravated the occurrence of malaria infection in the study area. The result from Table 4 shows that malaria is a disease that reoccurs if proper care and prevention is not taken.

PERCEIVED IMPACT OF MALARIA ON RESPONDENTS PRODUCTIVITY

To analyze the impact of malaria on productivity, the respondents were asked if malaria impacts on their productivity.

Table 5: Perceived Impact of Malaria on Respondents' Productivity

Categories	Frequency	Percentage (%)
Very severe	56	44.8
Fairly severe	48	38.4
Not quite severe	21	16.8
Total	125	100

Source: Field Survey, 2011.

From Table 5, out of the 125 respondents interviewed, 44.8 percent of the respondents claimed that malaria had a very severe impact on their productivity, while 38.4 percent reported that the impact of the disease was fairly severe. Less than 20 percent (16.8) said that the impact of malaria was not quite severe on their productivity. This finding has revealed that the majority of the inhabitants of Maiduguri would want to see the impact of malaria infection on their socioeconomic productivity as a seriously negative one.

LOSS OF LABOR HOURS (THE OPPORTUNITY COST OF MALARIA)

Malaria is a disease that has the ability to keep one away from work. It comes not without an opportunity cost. This is in form of labor hours lost because of malaria infection. Labor hour is also lost when members of the family stay away from work to take care of the sick. By the foregoing, it was found that hours lost to malaria in the study area amounted to about 77 percent of labor hours on the average. When this is estimated in monetary terms, the opportunity cost amounts to N147,970,000 for the 125 sampled population under study. This is shown in Table 6 below.

Table 6: Loss of Labor Hours (The Opportunity Cost of Malaria)

Categories	Mean monthly hours (pre-infection)	Mean monthly hours lost to malaria	Labor hours lost in %	Estimated income lost (monthly in N)
Business men/ women	432	89	19	67,900
Civil servants	320	106	33	67,320
Students	384	96	25	16,750
Total	1,136	282	77	147,970

Source: Field Survey, 2011.

From Table 6, it can be seen that a huge amount of productive hours are lost to malaria attacks. This results to low output and ultimately slows economic growth and development. This has a critical effect on the economy of Maiduguri as it reduces the income levels of households and thus their ability to save and invest.

The study tried to find the impact of malaria on personal income of the respondents. This is imperative in order to show the effect of malaria on income, thus its effect on savings and ultimately investment and other economic activities. To achieve this, the respondents were asked if there had been a reduction in their income during the period of malaria attack. This is shown in Table 7.

Table 7: The Perceived Impact of Malaria on Individual Income

Impact of malaria	Frequency	Percentage (%)
Significant Reduction	84	67.2
No significant reduction	30	24.0
Indifferent	11	8.8
Total	125	100

Source: Field Survey, 2011.

From Table 7 above, eighty-four respondents (67.2 percent of the sampled population) confirmed that there had been a significant reduction in their income during period of malaria attack, while thirty respondents (24.0 percent of the respondents) claimed that their income remained substantially unchanged during such malaria attack.

CONSOLIDATED MONETARY COST OF MALARIA

Table 8: Consolidated Monetary Cost of Malaria

Categories	Monthly expenses on treatment/ prevention of malaria	Income Loss (N)	Total
Business men/women	35,030	58,900	93,930
Civil servants	21758	67,320	89,078
Students	13,266	16,750	30,016
Total	70,054	147,970	513,024

Source: Field Survey, 2011.

For this study, the total sum lost to malaria amounts to an average of N513,024.00 per month by individuals. This gives to an average of about N5,000.00 per month for each individual under study as represented in Table 8 above. However, from Table 8, it can be seen that the labor income loss, which is the opportunity cost, is very much higher than the expenses on treatment and prevention. The implication of this is that the economy loses income level approximately above N5,000.00 every month per every inhabitant of Maiduguri Metropolis.

CONCLUSION

This empirical study has confirmed most of the views expressed in most relevant literature that Malaria is an endemic disease ravaging many sub-Saharan African cities—Maiduguri inclusive. Malaria is a disease that cuts across different social classes—peasants, civil servants, business men and women, students, artisans, etc. The study has confirmed that the labor hour lost to malaria infection with its attendant socioeconomic consequences on individuals and the general society call for government and all stakeholders urgent concern.

It was observed that malaria reduces productivity through labor hours lost. When labor hours lost to malaria is converted to monetary terms, it runs into hundreds of thousands of naira. This has an adverse effect on household income and standard of living as well as investment potentials.

The cost of malaria through hospitalization costs, purchase of drugs, preventive measures, etc., are so high in the study population. If this study is replicated in other urban and rural centers in Nigeria, the result might not be quite different.

RECOMMENDATIONS

Based on the findings of the paper, the following recommendations are made:

For proper control and ultimate eradication of malaria, there is a need to fight mosquitoes. This can be done by keeping the environments clean, clearing of refuse dumps, clearing of drainages and water logs, etc.

Government, i.e., federal, state, and local governments reintroduce aerial spray of insecticides in the study area. This can greatly prevent the people coming in contact with mosquitoes, hence reduction in cases of malaria.

There is also a need to get the people informed on the effects of malaria and how to prevent it. Most people are not aware of the need for them to properly treat malaria by seeing a qualified doctor. Collective or community control of malaria should be vigorously pursued.

Government should also provide proper health-care services to the people. Most people, especially the less privileged and uneducated, do not have access to proper health care. This could be related to high costs of health services and drugs. Government should provide health services and drugs to the people of Maiduguri at a subsidized rate. This will go a long way in reducing the incidence of declining economic activities as a result of malaria.

REFERENCES

Castilla, R. E. (1993*).* "Malaria Rate and Fate: A Socioeconomics Study of Malaria in Brazil." Universidade Federal De MinasGerais, CEDEPLHR, Belo Horonte MG-Brazil.

Chioma, R.I., Goodman, C.A., Mills A. (2003). "The Economic Impact of Malaria in Africa: A Critical Review the Evidence." www.nebi.n/m.nih.go.

David, R. (1997). "Larger Public Health Risk Overlooked in the Global Warming Debates." Respected Science organization.

Dhaka, M. (2000). "Impact of TB and Malaria on Poverty." A Paper Presented at a Conference of Parliamentarians on the Impacts of Tuberculosis and Malaria on Poverty.

Ettling, M.B. and Shepherd, D.C. (1991). *Economic Cost of Malaria in Rwanda.* Department of Population Science, Harvard School of Public Health, Boston, Massachusetts.

Foster S. (1998). "Economics and Its Contribution to the Fight Against Malaria." www.winterthurhealthforum.ch.

Malaney, P. (2003). "Microeconomic Approaches to Evaluating the Burden of Malaria" Institute of Medicine (IDM).

MFI (2000). "Ethiopia is Committed to Rollback Malaria." A Publication of the Malaria Foundation International.

Onwujekwe, O., China R., and Okonkwo, P. (2000*).* "Economic Burden of Malaria Illness on Households Versus That of All Other Illness Episode." A Study in Five Malaria Halo-Endemic Nigerian Communities. (WHO Year Book, 2000).

Roll Back Malaria (2000). "Abuja Declaration on Rollback Malaria in Africa."

Sachs J., and Maloney, P. (2002). "The Economic and Social Burden of Malaria." A Publication for International Development, John, F. Kennedy School of Government, Harvard University, Massachusetts USA.

Sajay, M. (2000). "400 Million Cases of Malaria Are Reported Every Year." Pan Africa Press Agency.

WHO (1997). "Malaria in Africa." WHO Year Book, 2002.

The Race of the Azerbaijani People in Iran (Atropatgan)

Vahid Rashidvash

*Department of Iranian Studies, Yerevan State University, Yerevan,
Armenia,
E-mail: vrashidvash@yahoo.com*

ABSTRACT

Asia continent as the largest and the most populous continent and the cradle of a developed civilization has different peoples with various races and with their special physical characteristics. The Iranian plateau as a special geographical place in Asia continent has had different nations with various races. Azerbaijan (Atropatgan) is one of the main and ancient places of Iran where it has Aryan residents. In this paper, attempt is made to study the race and people living there from the perspective of anthropology and ethnology. The origin of the Turkic-speaking population of the northwestern provinces of Iran, the so-called Azaris, is the subject of long-year debate. Here, we present preliminary results on testing of several hypotheses concerning their origin: the Azaris are the descendants of the Turkic ethnic groups migrated from Central Asia; they have an autochthonous origins; they are of Iranian origin; and they have mixed ethnic origin with unknown proportions of source populations' contribution.

Key Words: Atropatgan, Ethnology, Anthropology, Nations, Aryan race.

INTRODUCTION

The world is a place containing various racial and lingual groups. So that as far as this issue is concerned, there is no difference between developed and developing countries. As if, among all existing countries and islands in the world, about 160 countries have an increasing situation regarding race and culture. Iran is not an exception because it can be called a multinational or multiracial community. The Iranian plateau is a special geographical part of Asia continent containing Iran. This plateau is a mountainous and high place in the southwest of Asia with 2.600.000 kilometers or about 1.724.800 kilometers area. Iran is located in the southwest of Asia, in the Middle East with a 1.648.195 kilometers area. It is covered 63 percent of the Middle East (or two third), and the rest contains other countries. Iran was called Aran Shotor in Sasanid dynasty. In Achaemenian dynasty, it was named Iria. It was the name of an Iranian tribe. This word was applied by Caucasian nation as Irvoun-Ir-Irou. Some words such as Arians, Aria, Iran, and something like them are taken from that. Iran has been serving as an important bridge between the East and the West from many years ago, and main highways were crossed there connecting the civilizations of two sides. The great part of the Iranian plateau located between Indus and Oxus valley, Zagros and Caucasian mountains is Azerbaijan plateau (Atropatgan) in the north. Azerbaijan was covered by the Big Sea in the early of third era and called Titus. Consequently, great changes on the earth's crust, mountain-making movements, and volcanic actions have made the final geographical form of Azerbaijan plateau (Atropatgan) [1].

The effect of the natural and geographical form has affected the fate and historical events of this place. As for the business, this area was placed on the way of Caucasian commercial road and also the east-west path joined to Black Sea. And today, it is a gate to enter into the Europe.

Azerbaijan (Atropatgan) is one of the main and ancient provinces of Iran with Aryan people. Its name is taken from an old tribe, Atropatgan. Atro is Avestan and old pronunciation of Azar who was one of the Old Iranian goddesses and means the fire brightness. *Patik* means keeper and worshipper too. The name Atropatgan has been mentioned with other pronunciations in the ancient sources such as Atropaneh,

Atropatkan, Azerbaiganan, Azerbadgan, Azer Abadegan, Azerbaigan (the pronunciation of people in the Sasanian dynasty) Azerboijan, and Azerbaijan. Azerbaijan (Atropatgan) is one of the main and old centers of human's life. It has always been one of the most famous historical names in Iran with the oldness of 2,300 years and also one of the most valuable geographical places in Iran and the world. It has shown in different historical fields and produced famous figures too. Atropatgan is a large area to connect nations and a strong, patient, and talented race have settled here from past. That is why it is an important place on the view of anthropology, physiognomy, and even genetics.

THE RACE OF PEOPLE SETTLED IN THE IRANIAN PLATEAU

Race is applied to a group of people who have maintained a common physical or biological characteristic in successive generations [2]. Or a group of natural people inherited a common physical feature; they have the same race even with different languages and customs [3]. According to this definition, what makes it different between two races is physical inherent characteristics and nothing else. The early anthropologists tried to determine the multitypes nature of human by classification under the title of race based on geographical location and apparent characteristics as color and the other outward marks.

In 1350 BC, the scientists found physical differences among human populations and classified them into three groups with regard to the color (black, white. and yellow). The experts of heredity and biologists do not have a common idea about the reasons of variety in races. It means some of them know this difference resulted from heredity, and others believe in environmental effects [4]. In fact, the people of different places in the world are so mixed, and it seems unlikely to determine the exact racial location. It is not indeed out of ambiguity because the most anthropologists and scientists believe that human has always been exposed to immigration and racial integration. Racial integration is not only a historical reality but also in this active world; it is more intensive than the past. The nations' relations and repetitive marriages of different races during centuries and their continuous changes have caused no fixed race remains. It means that we cannot point to only one factor like color of skin to determine the race of a group. Other factors are considerable such as stature, the form of skull, head, hair, face, forehead, eyebrows, eyes, nose, and size of cheek, jaw, and also scattering of people on the base of blood group (genetics). Meanwhile, particularly the white race has had much integration with other races.

It is difficult for anthropologists and ethnologists to determine the race of people settled in the Iranian plateau. The reason is that it has been as an invasion field bilaterally from many years ago. On the other hand, it is as a bridge between the Far East, Middle East, and Mesopotamia. Therefore, many different nations with various races have entered this plateau and placed under a united ceiling of language. Anthropologists who study physical features are sure that some individuals with long heads have settled in Iran before the Nordic. But the related documents are few and imperfect. It seems that they have had a little relation with India. They had been Sumerians or related to them. It is still possible to find the sign of old Sumerians faces among people inherited in the southeast of Iran and Indus valley.

Generally, the main factors of Iranians are Mediterraneans. Moreover, there are some considerable varieties and deviations. In the Iranian plateau, people with extended heads are of two kinds: those with erect nose and some with big curved nose (every curved nose, less or much). The first group is probably related to Bedouins of the North Arabia, and the second have grown in the Iranian plateau. With the exception of this group, people with small heads used to live in Iran too. They are classified in three groups. The first group with erect nose, the second with so much curved and high parting of head, and the third with curved nose and extended faces and heads. Given the researches, the most important characteristic of people inherited in the plateau is that they have round head with ellipsoid faces. Now among people who live, especially in the east, there are individuals with round heads and extended faces. They live in heights and mountains more than valleys and plains. Some of them can be related to the Indian Dravidians because there are some people with round heads and ellipsoid faces. Tall stature and light color are their important features. It is resulted from intercourses with Nordic tribes. But regarding their light color, they can be known as Alp race. Moreover, today in Iran, there are northern and southern European kind, Mogul, Black, and Hamite.

The presence of these people in the form of Asian, European, and African shows the physical relations between Iran and the other three continents. There are some documents that indicate Iran has been a living place from the Stone Age. There were considerable amalgamations among different races resulted from extensive cultural relations and connections. Excavations and comparative studies have clarified it. It seems that the present residents in this plateau are more related to people in the west and the northwest of Iran. As a result of anthropological studies and measurements in Iran, one basic branch called "the white race" has been determined. It is the race of people in the Iranian plateau.

The ancient Iranians (Homo Iranicus) are the genius brothers of original mankind (Homo sapiens) grown in the southwest of Asia, physically and culturally, namely the cradle of direct ancestors of Aryans. The Iranians are among the oriental race called Indo-European who have immigrated to this plateau from Axus and Caucasian mountains in the late of the second thousand BC. They were called Aryan in the history. It took one thousand years for Aryans to enter into this plateau in different small and large groups. Finally, in the first millennium BC, they were replaced and then made various sovereignties. Some sects of oriental races entered Iran on the way of Caspian Sea has settled in the central Asia and Iranian plateau. The Parthians are among this group. A group of vanguards moved toward Indian valley. The western branch who passed into the north of Caspian Sea and entered Atropatgan on the way of Caucasian had a main role in the political and social life of the Iranians. They are the founders of Aryan Media and Achaemenian dynasty [5].

The Iranian plateau started a new life with fresh Aryan tribes and made the ancient age of Iran which lasts one thousand years. This time, it is regarded as the golden period in the history of Iran.

ETHNICAL GROUPS IN IRAN

At the present time, a nation can settle in a country with clear boarders or can be separated for historical events. Their races can be divided among some countries or can be scattered in different areas for immigrations [6]. There are some examples for the first and second types in the Middle East such as Iranians as a big nation in the past, Arabs, and the Turkish people. In Iran, with these geographical boarders, there are several nations in which their characteristics are presented in their race and language. Considering lingual dialects and geographical scattering, they have several branches.

According to lingual dialects, they are Turkish, Baluch, Kurd, Hyrcanian, Larestani, Lor, Azeri, and some others. Thus, this collection is applied to the Iranian nation. All of them have an Aryan and Iranian ethnical root, common past of one thousand years, history, culture, land inherit, and common language. None of them can be known as a separate nation. Although there are some differences between their dialects and languages, but lingual similarities are such that the collection of their dialects has made a common language as Persian language. This language cannot be related to any Iranian branch. It belongs to all Iranian people. Generally, there are three special races in Iran:

- Persians who have settled in Alborz and Zagros mountains in the south and the north to Sepid River. The Lors live in the west parts of Iran and have thick hair and lighter skin physically. Most of them are tall. Their skulls are pressed and round. They have an extended and a thin face. Their foreheads are a little big, have thick and semicircular eyebrows. Also the big, wide, lowly noses inclined to the ground. Their chins are inclined down and seem a little big. They have small cheeks with more distance between them. The hair color is as same as chestnut and have thick beard, unmixed race on the view of quality, and they are accounted among the Aryan race. The Kurds are the other group of Iranian nation settled in this area. There are three theories about their origin:

The first theory: They are among Indians and European races immigrated in the seventh century BC.

The second theory: It emphasizes on their native and lingual nature as if they know Kurds as the relatives of other Asian nations like Khaleds, Georgian, and Armenians.

The third theory: Kurd race is the diagram of Zagros, Gouti, Lolubi, Kasi, Orartouie, and other tribes who settled in Zagros or Kordestan in the past. They joined Indo-European nations and have the same race [7]. People in the southern parts of Iran have darker skin than usual Arabs in Iraq. Perhaps, they have the most rate of similarity with early people of the northern Arabia and desert of Syria regarding the color of skin. Evidently, there are individuals with dark skin too; but it does not cause any mistake with black people.

- People of Mazandaran and Guilan who are settled in the Caspian seaside villages separated from the Persians in Alborz valleys by the northern climate condition of Alborz. They are original Iranians. Their difference with Persians is resulted from the separation on the side of Alborz and geographical climate condition and not for race. They have medium stature with dark and pale appearance, black eyes, black and thick hair and beard.
- Azeri people who form all population of the northwestern and west of Iran are settled in a place called Azerbaijan (Atropatgan). Although there are some people with Persian language among them, but most of them are Turkish. It is worth mentioning that there are many differences between Iranian Turks and other Turkish nations. The Iranian Azeri people are not Turkish, unlike common beliefs, but they are original Iranians with Aryan race. Anthropological, genetics, and historical studies have proved this matter.

THE RACE OF ATROPATGAN PEOPLE

Today, there are a few nations whose ethnical amalgamation is not affected by immigrant nations. Since long time ago, different tribes have immigrated to find a better living place for various reasons such as looking for pastures, increasing population, natural revolutions, economical changes, or because of forces. They settled in a newer places, and it was likely that they had to change their places more than once. The northwest of Iran has been inhabited since the age of primitive people; some tribes emigrated from here to other places and sometimes returned to this place again. Therefore, it can be said that this area has been a passageway and a residential place for different nations.

This unique situation supports this opinion that Turkish people were among nations who have settled here from many years ago, and the beginning of their settlement is remained in the darkness of one thousand years. Consequently, in other words, we can consider them among the native people of this land. With the exception of native Turkish people, immigrant Turks have often passed here in subsequently periods, and some of them have settled in some parts. They have intermingled with their homolingual people, and after a while, some of them immigrated for invasions.

In the present historical sources, it is often talked about Turkish nations who sometimes passed from Caucasian passageway from the fifth century and came to south lands and Azerbaijan (Atropatgan). The subject discussed here is that some writers and archaeologists called them as Turk race in their studies and believe that the present inhabitants in Azerbaijan (Atropatgan) are from a Turk race. Their only reason is the language of these people. But their Turkish language is not a reason to be superior because race and culture are factors to make identity of the community, and language is itself a part of culture that is always changing. Thus, it has an insignificant role. In other words, language can never indicate race or nationality, and ethnical union is only based on common race, history, and culture.

One of the main ways to determine race is skull. Skull is a bone case that contained brain and special senses and is responsible to keep them. Skull itself is made of different bones including frontal, back of head, temporal, and molar bones [8]. It is possible to determine the race of a person completely by the exact studying of skull by different tools in comparison and contrast with others skull and even with the skeletal remains from past. Measuring the parts of the body and skull is completely practical, and we can determine the form of the body by obtained numbers. Certainly, the numbers to classify the race depend on the individual's desire and invention; for example, a skull can be measured ten or one thousand times. The recognition of racial characteristics is a little difficult because there is no information related to craniology of early inhabitants in Atropatgan, unless there are some ancient documents.

Given the explorations and discoveries of bones from early people in Atropatgan, we can discuss about individuals' skulls in this area. These bones belong to native inhabitants. As a result of studies and measuring these skulls and also based on anthropological studies, it is obtained that people in this area have a rather round heads. It means that the upper part of skull, called tinsel in medical, is round and has no special projection. Thus, frontal bone begun from its attachment place to forehead bone and then inclined as semicircle with 100 degrees or 105 degrees downward and to the back of skull and attaches to the forehead bone. The state of semicircle in obtained bones in mentioned area has proven this matter that inhabitants' skulls are round, and it is one of the main characteristics of Aryans. The state of being round affects on the form of face bones, particularly on the cheek, eye, socket, and nose. It has caused that face bone becomes big, extended, and ellipsoid. Forehead bone is a little big, protuberant, extended, and smooth. Eye socket is big, square, semicircle, or round. Of course, in some skulls, eye sockets are different on the view of smallness and bigness. The nostrils are wide and big. The width between the arches of molar bones is one of the main characteristics, especially that much width may show intermingling with the Moguls and Turks. Therefore, cheek can be one of the other differences between Turks and resident people in Atropatgan (Azerbaijan of Iran) namely Aryans. Molar bone (Oz Zygomaticum) is placed on the sides to make protuberant.

After studying the cheek of inhabitant people in Atropatgan, it was determined that they have delicate and narrow cheeks. But the Moguls and Turks have wide and big cheeks. This difference is clearer in Aryans and Turks by the color of skin. Chin bone is lowly and extended, and face is ellipsoid. Thus, it has a great effect on the chins and cheeks. It means that superior maxilla bone is big and lowly because of cheek smallness. This bigness is completely observable in the inferior maxilla bone. Now we proceed to apparent characteristics of inhabitant people in this area. As a result of field studies in Atropatgan, the following outcomes have been obtained:

People in this area have white or whitened or to some extent brown and a little dark skin. According to this research, 95 percent of residents in mountainous areas, especially in Shand Heights, have a white or light color as if we can point to Kandovan village in south of Azerbaijan (Atropatgan). In the northwest of this area, white or even dark and whitened people are observed. In Ahar Township in the west of Azerbaijan, the white and yellow races are observed among men and women. They are often mongrel. Certainly, there are individuals who are dark black and green, but most of them are immigrant and have come here from other areas. However, generally, Atropatgan inhabitants are white.

The size of head is the most important difference between people in Azerbaijan and other races. In other nations, head is round. It has caused ellipsoid faces in this area as if the length of face is a little more than its width. People of Azerbaijan have small and semicircle heads on the view of length. The width of their head is less and narrow. The width and length of the head are a little different in cities and villages, but it is not significant.

In the course of the researches, some people with extended heads in the northwest of Iran have been observed. Thus, given this point, we can classify the present inhabitants into two types: those with long and round heads and those with round head.

Their characteristics are as the following:

Characteristics of those with extended heads:

- Extended head and long hair, big, curved, and narrow nose (every curved nose, less or much), narrow face;

- Extended head and face of Mediterranean, erect nose, square maxilla;
- Extended head, small face of Mediterranean, erect and a rather wide nose and square maxilla;
- The intercourse of one and two that may be Nordic.

Characteristics of those with round head:

- Round head, square maxilla with curved or erect nose of early Alp;
- Long parting of head and smooth center of Armenia with curved nose.

Samples and measurements of head for size and form in Azerbaijan (Atropatgan) approve this point that two-thirds of individuals have round head and the rest, medium and ellipsoid. Those with ellipsoid heads have round face too. They are probably results from intercourse with Turks. Others who have round head are accounted among Aryans regarding to head criteria.

In the north of Azerbaijan, people have brownish black hair. Gray hair can be observed rarely before forty years old. The color of hair in 60 percent of Azeris's (Atropatgan) is between black and brown. Ninety percent of those people have thick hair, and generally, it is straight. Given to hair tissue, 40 percent has soft and others, medium and minority bristles. There are a few bald ones, resulted from old age or illness. Most of people have full-beard faces. Their beard is black or dark brown. In the east of Azerbaijan, people have generally black or dark brown hair. Concerning color and given to the type, there is any kind of hair from soft to bristles, but most have soft.

People have high, wide, big, smooth, and extended foreheads. The length of forehead is to some extend more, and its width is not completely extended. Most of the time, it is wrinkled and have grown well. People in these areas have mostly thick eyebrows, and even sometimes, it has covered top of the nose. But there are separate eyebrows too. They have had semicircular, extended, and a little curved form. ninety-five percent have curved, 80 percent thick, 15 percent ordinary, and 5 percent have separate eyebrows. But these features (curved and round) are seen among people.

Eyes are, to some extent, round and generally brown. A few of them have brown-green, and most of them have brown-blue eyes too. Only a few ones have had reddish brown eyes. The light colors indicate the factor of blond among them. Totally, it can be said that 84 percent have dark brown, 15 percent conical, and some have lighter eyes. White part of the eyes is clear in most, and a few have albugo. The distance between eyes vertically and also the distance of eyebrows with eye horizontally is small. During the researches, some individuals who have had extended, and long eyes were observed. They are a few but are not accounted among Aryans ethnically and perhaps have Mogul or Turk race affected by ethnical intercourse during the time.

One of the most important physical features to determine a race is the length, the width, and the profile of nose. With regard to the size, nose is big and a little smooth. It means that 80 percent of people have big and extended noses. Tip of nose is wide and lowly inclined to ground, and others have medium, and a few have small and delicate noses observed in more women. However, the nose size makes unusual appearance especially when it is seen sideways. People settled in the south of Azerbaijan (Atropatgan) have medium noses, and about half of them have curved, and more than one-third have erect noses. In the west, the profile of nose has a considerable variety. But most of them are curved and big, and a few are erect. In the studies, some people with erect and small noses are seen too. They are short and have more extended head, round face, narrower forehead, wider maxilla, and smaller nose. People with extended heads, on the contrary, with round head ones have small, narrow, and delicate noses. On the opposite, round-head ones have big, extended, lowly, and broken noses that are a feature of Aryans.

The lip and mouth concerning the size, the lips are medium but in some cases large and a little turned. Through researches, someone with turned lips has been observed. It was seen among the inhabitants of villages, more or less. Seemingly, length and width of ear does not have ethnical importance. The size of the ear in different cities is not the same. In some cases, nose was very small, big or extended; but in an overall view, it can be said that residents in this area have short and smaller ears as compared with other ethnical groups like Turk and Mogul. A few had big ears observed in the studies. But this bigness was not so much as if we account them among other races. The maximum width of external ear has a close relation with its length, and that is the fact that both will increase by age.

We cannot give a special opinion about stature. Maximum is between one hundred sixty or one hundred ninety centimetres, and more than half are classified as medium. Moreover, there was a considerable variety. It has no unusual variety while sitting, and it indicates the equal size between body and foot length.

Regarding the body, those who live near mountains are often thin, but they have strong muscles. Their hands and legs are elegant and a little big and rough because of job, particularly farming.

Let it not remain unsaid that there are Arab Iranian race among Azeri too. In the year 21 AH when Arabs came into Iran, the first ethnical amalgamation happened. Azerbaijan (Atropatgan) and original Aryan Iranians in this area were not deprived from this ethnical amalgamation. As if 25 percent has this race, but 5 percent has unmixed Arab race and 15 percent mongrel (Arab Iranian). They have special genealogies for themselves. They have the same typology with people settled in this area. Although this amalgamation took place, Aryan race has been superior because of being a dominant race. Moreover, they may have insignificant differences with Aryans. Their most important features are white color, blue, and bluish green eyes, blond hair, black eyes with high forehead, curved eyebrows, extended and lowly nose, and black hair.

Conclusion

Considering the studies about unique features of people in Atropatgan, we came to this conclusion that Atropatgan inhabitants have Aryan race like other Iranians. As a result, if they were from other race like Turks, they would be yellow as Turkish people. In fact, the investigation clarifies that they are not yellow. The reason is that among people settled in Atropatgan, none of the features related to yellow race in north is observed such as yellow skin, thin and extended eyebrows, oval eyes, and big protuberant cheeks. They are the most obvious characteristics of Turkish people.

All the characteristics are observed in all groups of Turks and yellow race in the north as Kyrgyzstani, Cossak, Uzbek, and mostly in Turkmen. But on the opposite, not only the features of white race are observed in Atropatgan like big eyes, white skin, and nonprotuberant cheeks, but most of them still have special characteristics of Aryan, such as light eyes and hair even after many years of Arab and Turk invasions.

It is worth noting that because of the history of the region, political changes in different parts of Iran, invasion of Turk, Mogul, and Arab, Atropatgan inhabitants are homogeneous as race is concerned. The invasion of nomads into Iran and Mogul penetration, hostility and long fighting with Ottoman, and their penetration to Atropatgan have caused changes in the nature of this Aryan country concerning its history and its identity. Therefore, the manifestation of the change appeared in the language of people in this area and not in their race. In fact, they have remained original Aryans because of the lack of human actions and reactions.

According to the two-thousand-five-hundred-year-history of Iran, Atropatgan inhabitants have been considered as Iranians and united with all of them. They are known as Iranian nation, and we cannot consider any new race for these people. The race of people in Atropatgan has been the same as Iranians from the beginning. Azerbaijan inhabitants (Atropatgan) are among the most original and the oldest Iranian families, namely Aryan race. They have kept all Iranian characteristics in Achaemenidae, Arsacides, and Sassanid dynasties and so far kept their ethnical nobility. Through history, particularly in the contemporary history, Atropatgan has been the pioneer of progressing social and political movements and intellectual events in Iran. Therefore, knowing them as non-Aryan on the view of ethnical characteristics is completely rejected. Moreover, all the documents indicate that they are Aryan. They are the reminders and grandchildren of Aryan and Parse Medes. All Kurds, Lors, and Iranian races are their reminders. Atropatgan inhabitants are the real generation and heritors of their ancestors' race, namely Aryans.

REFERENCES

Darvish zadeh, Ali. (2002). *Geology of Iran*, first edit, Tabriz, Niya pub.

Diakunef, Igor Mikhailouvich. (2004) *Medes History*. Translated by Karim Keshavarz. 7th ed. Scientific and Cultural Publication.

Fakuhi, Naser. (2006). *Anthropological Parts*. First edit, Tehran, Ney Publication.

Hastrup, Karisten. (1995). *A Passage to Anthropology, Between Experience and Theory*, London.

Hunter, David E. and Philip Whitten. (1976). *The Study of Anthropology*, New York.

Safizadeh, Sedigh. (1999). *History of Kurd and Kurdestan*, first edit, Tehran, Atiyeh publ.

Saidiyan, Abd Alhossein. (1991). *Peoples of the World*, 4th ed. Tehran, Science and Life Publication.

Sobbota, Becher. (2001). *Atlas of Human Anatomy*, vol 2, Urban and Schwarzenberg.

The Latent Dilemma of African Writers: A Socio-Anthropological Criticism of Achebe's Things Fall Apart

Joyce M. Edwards, Virginia State University
Zacchaeus Ogunnika, Virginia State University.

INTRODUCTION

This paper critically analyses Achebe's *Things Fall Apart* in order to determine his treatment of the African personality and the place given to African culture in the book. The paper is not attempting to romanticize African culture, neither is it an attempt to evade self-criticism of the African culture by the African literary artists. Rather, it attempts to point out some of the "seen but not always noticed" characteristics in some African writers. These kinds of writers always present the historical analysis of cultural contact with the European and try to explain the process of African culture. Such works as epitomized in *Things Fall Apart* always identify the presence of tension and conflict during the initial contact but portray African culture as not well equipped to deal with such a situation. This always resulted into a loss on the part of the African culture because "things always fell apart" in times of external assault.

The most disturbing part of such books is how they always present the African personality, social behavior, and group psychology. African heroes identified in such books are presented as being stupid, inhuman, and wicked. In many parts of such books, Africans are presented as being stupid, primitive, and uncivilized. This can be detected in *Things Fall Apart* when Abame people were presented as so foolish to the extent of not being able to distinguish between a horse and a bicycle which they called an iron horse.

All these are what the paper calls the "ridiculing of the self to amuse others" or an "underdog mentality" in some African writers. Achebe's *Things Fall Apart* is not the only book in this line of thought, but we shall utilize the book to advance our argument about African writers who display African culture within the mentality described in this paper.

SOCIO-ANTHROPOLOGICAL LITERARY CRITICISM

The socio-anthropological conception of literary works is that they are based on historical facts, past and present. They are, therefore, not conceived from a vacuum.

Iyasere's (1975) assertion that most African writers, among many things, attempt to use their works as storehouse of petrified ethnographic "truth" seems to lend credence to the belief of the socio-anthropologists. This author agrees with the socio-anthropologists' belief that most writers present the accounts of the social reality of their immediate environment, turning it into literary form by their excellent power of language usage. Some authors, in addition to their presentation of the account of the past-social reality, also present their vision of future reality. These are the writers who "predict" what they hope would happen in the future. Literary criticisms based on socio-anthropological perspectives, which is the approach of this paper, are digging deep into the actual critique—origin of the work in question. Such criticism cannot just be dismissed merely as a nonliterary approach to the literary work. Socio-anthropological literary criticism approaches a literary work from the standpoint of the meaning it conveys and is equally (if not more) as important as the criticism based upon the usage of language and writing skills which some writers seem to be advocating. This paper is therefore utilizing the socio-anthropological perspective to examine Achebe's *Things Fall Apart* from the standpoint of the meaning the work conveys.

Explaining Social Changes

One of the most frequent arguments adduced to support themselves by writers who present the kind of work described earlier is that they are presenting an objective fact. They also assert that their novels represent a creative writer's effort to explain social change as it has actually happened. In addition, they affirm that the writers were trying to document, through a literary artist's eyes, the evils of colonialism in Africa. Our contention here is that such presentations are not always accurate writers, such as Achebe, add and/or remove some vital facts to make such work acceptable to their foreign audience. But most sophisticated and sometimes casual readers of novels understand that novels are written within a specific sociocultural environment. Such readers are not always aware that such writers have removed or included it in order to wet their appetite to read the books. They therefore believe that what they find in the novels represents real and accurate information about the specific society. It should also be noted that literary works are not produced in a vacuum. They are born out of an original idea which the author has been harboring and wanted to release. Most authors used their books to propagate and promote a cause by distorting reality. Achebe's book is doing exactly this because we believe he was promoting the cause of the victory of modernism over tradition and Christianity over what he believed to be African Fetish Religion. His account in the book *Things Fall Apart* could therefore not be said to be an account of social change nor the documentation of the obvious. His presentation of the Igbo people as those who easily succumbed to the invading white culture and religion, in my opinion, is not fair to the Igbo people in particular and Africans generally. *Things Fall Apart* in the opinion of this author is too much biased against the Igbo. Achebe's account of the ease with which the white missionaries and the new converts conquered the "evil forest" showed the weakness of the Igbo traditional religion compared to that of the white man.

Imagine this statement from the book, "And then it became known that the white men's fetish had unbelievable power, it was said that he wore glasses on his eyes so that he could talk to evil spirits." After this event, whereby African religion was humiliated, the book said that the white man won their first three converts. To this author, Achebe demonstrated to the reader in that statement that immediately the African came in contact with the white man, he (the African) became disillusioned about his own religion, power, and knowledge which (African) believed were inferior to that of the white man. Our argument is not bothering on whether the converts were not won over, nor were the victory on the evil forest unreal, but we hold that the victory could not have been as easy as Achebe portrayed. African power, knowledge, and technology did not just fall like packs of cards when this culture was invaded. Contemporary evidence still shows the power of Africa's past. This has prompted advocates for creating a department for the study of African traditional knowledge in our higher institutions.

Another account which shows the incompetence of African culture and personality in the book is Achebe's explanation of how the government of the white man was established. Could we say this is saying the obvious through a literary artist's view? The book, though, not writing history but utilizing history as a storehouse for where knowledge is gathered, presented the situation as one in which the government was established without any resistance by the Africans.

This should be far from being the truth because historical evidence depicts that in no part of Nigeria was the European system of government established without a resistance. The Nigerians of the past did not only resist the European government but also resented their presence. It was on record that the resistance of the European by Africans was so enormous that European had to resort to numerous wars and expeditions to bring the people's compliance which eventually did not come. History also recorded the facts that in most of their wars, the white invaders suffered lots of misfortunes, setbacks, and death as could be seen in Benin under King Overami and Abeokuta under the *Egba* United Government. It was on record that the British who brought government to Nigeria were second-generation invaders. The Portuguese came to Africa before them and could not colonize the people nor introduce their (Portuguese) form of government.

If the Africans were so weak, the Portuguese who blazed the trail before the British should have introduced a government. The success of the British in establishing a government might be related to their double dealing and treachery. Seen in the domain of meaning and situated historically, *Things Fall Apart* was narrating a story which took place in the mid-19th Century when the whites were no longer "new" in Africa. How come then that Achebe should present them (the Africans) as being so stupid in acting as if they were seeing the white men for the first time? Evidence abounds to suggest that the white man was not so much feared by the Africans as the book portrayed him. Imagine what Sultan Bello told Lugard at the turn of the century:

> *"Between us (Africans) and you (Whiteman) there are no*
> *dealings except as between Mussulmans and the unbelievers.*
> *War as the God Almighty enjoined us."*

That was in 1902. In *Things Fall Apart,* we were only told that the white men brought the government, but the author failed to explain how it really happened. However, historians narrated the tricks and treacherous ways surrounding the signing of treaties and the strong resistance by the then Africans.

The story about the destruction of Abame is equally alarming as well as disturbing. This author finds it hard to believe that the level of sophistication of Igbo society at that time was as it was portrayed. We believe that judging by the circumstances surrounding the story, *Things Fall Apart* was based on the nineteenth-century episode of the contact with the white man. Could an Igbo man be so ignorant of a white man in the eighteenth century to the extent of running away from him (white man)? Igbo would certainly have got contact with the Portuguese who come in the thirteenth century. Achebe's account here looked as a replay of Haggard's *King Solomon's Mines* in which the author portrays the Kukuana people as being so unsophisticated to the extent of referring to the white men as "people from the moon" despite the fact that they (the Kukuanas) even noticed a black man among the whites. How can one be comfortable with a book which says that the Igbo society mistook a bicycle for a horse in the nineteenth century? This analogy cannot be symbolic as can be understood in the way the book itself put it:

> "A white man appeared in their clan . . . And he was riding an
> iron horse . . . And so they killed the white man and tied his

> iron horse to their sacred tree *because it looked as if it will run away to call the man's friends."*

This is an unfair analogy. If an analogy is made between a donkey and a horse or even a cat and a horse, it would have been fairer. The mere fact that the bicycle was tied to a tree so that "it might not run away" betrayed the intention of the author, which is only to amuse his readers. I am of the opinion that it is not fair to ridicule one's own culture merely to amuse others which might result in high sales for the book. It can only be compared with Haggard's account in *King Solomon's Mines* when Kukuanas believed that a gun was a "pipe which kills from a distance." Achebe also has the love of ridiculing Africans when acting as a group. This could be detected in his account of Abame's destruction which showed that the Igbo should be blamed for what happened to them. Achebe blamed the people of Abame for causing their own problem by "touching a man (white) who said nothing." This area was included by Achebe to win customers from the white world. It show that writers like Gunder Frank and Rodney were wrong on their account of how Europe underdeveloped Africa. If properly translated, all the theories of colonialism, exploitation of the underdeveloped, and that of imperialism and dependency are wrong. Africans are portrayed as causing their own problems as revealed in this passage from the book: "Never kill a man who says nothing. Those men of Abame are fools." If Achebe was presenting an account of social change from the literary artist's point of view, then he was "blaming the victim." Blaming the victim is a situation in which one presents the affected as the cause of his own misfortunes. I believe there are other ways of presenting social change from a literary artist's point of view which might not necessarily blame the victim or romantice the victim.

Such an approach is detected in Laye's *The Radiance of the King* in which, according to Izevbaye, he (Laye) "uses the usual stereotypes about 'primitive' Africa to glorify her in a deliberate ironic manner." Ngugi's *Weep Not Child* is also a novel which described a process of change in Kenya without blaming the African. The book (Ngugi's) retained the pride of the African throughout. I am even tempted to confess that I feel more at home with the writings based on the negritude orientation, whatever the critics of such writers might say, when compared to Achebe's writings.

This paper is not examining Achebe personality as a writer. Our argument, however, is that each book which is written by any writer has its own specific message. It is the message contained in *Things Fall Apart* that we are attempting to analyze. Nobody, unless the professional creative arts, would have to wait until he has finished reading all Achebe's work before translating what he has read in any of his books to mean his (Achebe's) picture of social reality.

J. P. O'Flinn pointed out that a novelist has to be assured of the existence of several thousand potential buyers before writing his book. All these buyers cannot necessarily be literary artists. We therefore object to the place given to African culture in *Things Fall Apart* because these potential, nonsophisticated readers include those who are having their first contact with African culture through the book. That this statement is almost true can be inferred from O'Flinn's contention that if a literary artist's work is to be consumed locally, "a sizeable percentage of its population must both be literate and has an income sufficiently high to make the purchase of books feasible." O'Flinn then believes that the Nigerian novelists are "not really catering for Nigeria but are using outlets providing by international publishers to address a largely non-African, let alone non-Nigerian audience." He therefore advices that novelists should not only think of amusing these non-African audience as Achebe did in *Things Fall Apart* but must try to sincerely educate and inform their audience about the facts of African culture. The first part of *Things Fall Apart* was very educative, interesting, and full of in-depth knowledge of the Igbo people, culture, and aspiration. It presented the Igbo society, its achievement orientation system, and its group solidarity. But things began to fall apart in the novel as from part II when the white men came with the new religion, and the Igbos were presented as acting as the "underdogs" in most of their interactions with these "Strangers" (white men).

There was a big contrast between Achebe's presentation here and that of Ngugi in *Weep Not, Child*. In all their confrontation with the white men, the Africans in Ngugi's book always act like "brave men." Instead, in Achebe's book, Okonkwo who was trying to retain his self-pride as an African was presented as a deviant, not only through the eyes of others (white men) but also through the eyes of his own people. This is confirmed by the statement made after he (Okonkwo) has committed suicide to show that he was no more accepted by his own people. The Igbo people commented that owing to this disgraceful behavior of Okonkwo, "he would be buried like a dog." This author believes that the misfortune of Okonkwo could have been presented in a more dignified manner so as to reflect the real tradition of the Africans. Misfortunes are also recorded in Ngugi's *Weep Not, Child,* but the victims, be they Africans or others, are not so shabbily treated as Achebe presented Okonkwo. An example is the murder of Jacobo and the tragedy of Ngotho's family which Ngugi did not present us with a story that makes us laugh about the stupidity of an African who refused to change but, instead, presented us with the tragedy of an African who understood the situation but was struggling not to be swallowed by the inhumanity of the white man who, after all, was a stranger in his own home.

In all, this essay believes in the enormous power of the literary artists to propagate the African culture. The extent and the extensive area of circulation covered by their novels readily make them to be agents which could disseminate ideas about the African culture through their books. We, therefore, believe that a creative artist's writings should have more in them than merely amusing people in order to sell their books. African writers must try to be agents of African development, and they must be patriotic. A writer who engages in what Onoge calls a "negative self-accounting of national character" would not help this and the unborn generation to acquire the much-needed self-confidence which is an essential factor in African development.

References

Adeleye, R., *Power and Diplomacy in Northern Nigeria: The Sokoto Caliphate and Its Enemies.* New York: Humanities Press, 1971.

Achebe Chnua. *Things Fall Apart.* London, Ibadan: Nairobi: Heinemann Educational Book.

Awolowo Obafemi. *The People's Republic.* Ibadan, Oxford University Press, 1968.

Garfinkel Harold *Studies in Ethnomethodology*, Englewood, NJ: Prentice Hall Inc., 1976.

Ivor Frederick Case "Negritude and Utopianism" in E. O. Jones ed. *African Literature Today* in Durosimi Jones (ed.). African Literature Today. London Ibadan: Heinemann.

Nduka Otonti Western Education and the Nigerian cultural background. Ibadan: Oxford University Press, 1975.

O'Flinn, J. P. "Toward Sociology of Nigeria Novels" in Durosimi Jones (ed.). African Literature Today. London Ibadan: Heinemann.

Ngugi Wa Thiong'o. *Weep Not, Child*. London, Ibadan, Nairobi-Heinemann, 1966.

Iyasere Solomon Ogbeide. "African Critic on African Literature: A study in Eldred" Durosimi Jones ed. African Literature Today. London Ibadan: Heinemann, 1975.

Onoge Omafume, F. "On Cultural Configuration of the Current Crisis." A paper presented at the ASSU National Conference on the State of the National Economy, 1984.